Information Security Law:
The Emerging Standard for
Corporate Compliance

Information Security Law: The Emerging Standard for Corporate Compliance

THOMAS J. SMEDINGHOFF

IT Governance Publishing

IT Governance Publishing
IT Governance Limited
Unit 3, Clive Court
Bartholomew's Walk
Cambridgeshire Business Park
Ely
Cambridgeshire
CB7 4EH
United Kingdom

www.itgovernance.co.uk

First published in the United Kingdom in 2008
by IT Governance Publishing.

ISBN 978-1-905356-66-9

PREFACE

This book is designed to provide an overview to the law of information security and the standard for corporate compliance that appears to be developing worldwide. It is based on a review of numerous security statutes and regulations, and the resulting realization that there is an amazing consistency in approach among most laws and regulations governing corporate information security obligations. It seeks to explain that approach.

It takes a high level view of security laws and regulations, and summarizes the global legal framework for information security that emerges from those laws. As such, it does not seek to address how to comply with the details of any specific security law or regulation. Instead, it is written from the perspective of a company that needs to comply with many laws in many jurisdictions, and needs to understand the overall framework of legal security requirements, so it can evaluate how local law fits in, and what it might do to become generally legally compliant in many jurisdictions and under many laws.

The basic approach is to look at global security laws and regulations as a group, in order to discern the trends and overall requirements for compliance from that perspective. This will give companies a broad view of the nature of their legal obligations, and a framework for understanding individual laws they must address. While the scope and applicability of security laws varies widely from one law to the next, and from one jurisdiction to the next, this high level view of the body of information security law should help companies better understand the overall nature of legal obligations relating to security, and how best to comply.

To that end, footnotes are used rather extensively to provide references to some of the various laws and regulations. However, they are primarily intended to identify examples of laws addressing a particular point, and should not be viewed as a complete list of all such laws. An Appendix lists many of these often-cited security laws and regulations.

ABOUT THE AUTHOR

Thomas J. Smedinghoff is a partner in the Privacy, Data Security, and Information Law Practice at the law firm of Wildman, Harrold, Allen & Dixon LLP in Chicago. His practice focuses on the developing field of information law and electronic business activities, with an emphasis on information security and privacy issues, electronic transactions, and the corporate use and management of information generally.

Mr Smedinghoff has been actively involved in developing e-business and information security legal policy, both in the US and globally. He currently serves as a member of the US Delegation to the United Nations Commission on International Trade Law (UNCITRAL) Working Group on Electronic Commerce, where he participated in negotiation of the 2005 *United Nations Convention on the Use of Electronic Communications in International Contracts*. He chaired the Illinois Commission on Electronic Commerce and Crime (1996-1998) that wrote the *Illinois Electronic Commerce Security Act*. He also served as an American Bar Association advisor to the Uniform Law Commission, where he participated in drafting the *Uniform Electronic Transactions Act* (UETA) now enacted in 46 of the 50 states in the US.

Mr Smedinghoff currently chairs the International Policy Coordinating Committee of the American Bar Association (ABA) Section of Science & Technology Law. Previously, he was chair of the ABA Section of Science & Technology Law (1999-2000) and chair of the ABA Electronic Commerce Division (1995-2003).

About the Author

He is also the editor and primary author of the e-commerce book titled *Online Law: The Legal Guide to Doing Business on the Internet* (1996).

He can be reached at smedinghoff@wildman.com.

TABLE OF CONTENTS

INTRODUCTION

Information security is rapidly emerging as one of the most critical legal issues facing companies today. As the list of highly-publicized security breaches suffered by very reputable companies, organizations, and government agencies continues to expand at an exponential rate, it is becoming very clear that the vulnerability of all corporate data is, in many respects, a time bomb waiting to explode.

The legal and public policy focus on information security stems from the fact that, in today's business environment, virtually all of a company's daily transactions and all of its key records are created, used, communicated, and stored in electronic form using networked computer technology. Most business entities are, quite literally, fully dependent upon information technology and an interconnected information infrastructure.

This has, of course, provided companies with tremendous economic benefits, including significantly reduced costs and increased productivity. But the resulting dependence on electronic records and a networked computer infrastructure also creates significant potential vulnerabilities that can result in major harm to the business and its stakeholders.[1] Creating, communicating, and storing corporate information in electronic form greatly enhances the potential for unauthorized access, use,

---

[1] "As a result of increasing interconnectivity, information systems and networks are now exposed to a growing number and a wider variety of threats and vulnerabilities. This raises new issues for security." OECD Guidelines for the Security of Information Systems and Networks, July 25, 2002, p. 7, available at www.oecd.org/dataoecd/16/22/15582260.pdf.

disclosure, and alteration, as well as the risk of accidental loss or destruction.

Concerns regarding corporate governance, individual privacy, accountability for financial information, the authenticity and integrity of transaction data, and the protection of sensitive business data are driving the enactment of laws and regulations designed to ensure that businesses adequately address the security of their own data. These legislative and regulatory initiatives are imposing obligations on all businesses to implement information security measures to protect their own data and to disclose breaches of security that do occur.

In particular, businesses need to understand and address three legal trends that are rapidly shaping the global information security landscape, and defining the requirements that businesses must satisfy. They are:

- an expanding duty to provide security for corporate data;
- the emergence of a legal standard for compliance; and
- the imposition of a new duty to warn those adversely affected by a security breach.

While the law is still developing, and is often applied only in selective areas, these trends are posing significant new challenges for most businesses. This book will examine the law of information security in these three areas.

CHAPTER 1: SECURITY BASICS: THE LEGAL PERSPECTIVE

The law of information security is based on fundamental security concepts long recognized by security professionals. Thus, understanding security obligations from a legal perspective requires understanding those basic security concepts. The following sections will summarize those security concepts, as seen from the perspective of applicable laws.

1.1 Definition of information security

Security is the protection of assets (such as buildings, equipment, cargo, inventory, and in some cases, people) from threats. "Information security is the protection of information from a wide range of threats in order to ensure business continuity, minimize business risk, and maximize return on investments and business opportunities."[2]

Information security is also sometimes referred to as computer security, cybersecurity, or information assurance. Regardless of the label, it focuses on the protection of information systems and the data, messages, and information that are typically processed, communicated, and stored on such information systems. It is "the process by which an organization protects and secures systems,

---

[2] ISO/IEC 27002:2005, *Information Technology – Security Techniques – Code of Practice for Information Security Management* (June 2005), p. viii (hereinafter "ISO27002"); copies of this standard can be purchased from www.itgovernance.co.uk/standards.aspx .

media, and facilities that process and maintain information vital to its operations."[3]

The corporate *information systems* to be protected include the computers, communication networks, storage media, software, firmware, services, and related resources that are used to acquire, store, process, manage, communicate and transmit data or information.[4]

The *information* to be protected includes a wide variety of data, such as personally identifiable information about employees, customers, prospects, and other individuals, corporate financial information, information regarding corporate business transactions, trade secrets and other confidential information, information relating to corporate communications, including e-mail, and a variety of other types of corporate data. It can also take a variety of forms, including data, messages, documents, voice recordings, images, video, software, and other content in both electronic and paper form.

The various *threats*[5] to information and information systems, where they come from, what is at risk, and how serious the consequences are, will vary greatly from case to case. This is one of the key facts driving the legal approach to information security discussed in Chapters 4, 5, and 6.

The means used to provide protection from such threats are referred to as *security controls*.[6] They are the policies, processes, procedures, organizational structures, hardware

---

[3] FFIEC, *IT Examinations Handbook – Information Security* (July 2006) at p. 1, available at www.ffiec.gov/ffiecinfobase/booklets/information_security/information_security.pdf.
[4] See e.g. US Homeland Security Act of 2002, Section 1001(b), amending 44 USC § 3532(b)(4); HIPAA Security Regulations, 45 CFR Section 164.304.
[5] See Section 1.3.
[6] See Section 1.4.

devices, and software established and implemented to deter, detect, and respond to threats.

1.2 Objectives of information security

The law typically defines requirements for information security in terms of the objectives to be achieved. In some cases, statutes and regulations define those objectives in terms of positive results to be achieved, such as ensuring the *confidentiality, integrity, and availability* of information.[7] In other cases, they define those objectives in terms of the harms to be avoided – e.g. to protect systems and information against unauthorized access, use, disclosure or transfer, modification or alteration, processing, and accidental loss or destruction.[8]

Some laws and regulations combine both approaches. For example, one US federal law defines information security as follows:

---

[7] See e.g. US GLB Security Regulations (OCC), 12 CFR Part 30 Appendix B, Part II.B; HIPAA Security Regulations, 45 CFR Section 164.306(a)(1); Argentina Act, Section 9(2); Estonia Act, Section 19(1); Italy Act, Annex B, Section 19.4; Liechtenstein Ordinance, Article 9.

[8] Most privacy laws in other countries adopt this perspective for their security requirements. This includes, for example, the EU Data Protection Directive, Article 17(1); Albania Act, Article 9; Argentina Act, Article 9(1); Australia Act, Schedule 3, Section 4.1; Austria Act, Section 14(1); Belgium Act, Art. 16(4); Canada Act, Schedule 1, Section 4.7.1; Denmark Act, Section 41(3); Estonia Act, Section 19(1) and (2); Finland Act, Section 32(1); France Act, Article 34; German Act, Annex (to the first sentence of Section 9), Sections 1, 2, and 4; Greece Act, Article 10(3); Hong Kong Act, Principle 4; Hungary Act, Article 10(2); Ireland Act, Section 2-(1)(d), and First Schedule, Article 7; Italy Act, Section 31; Lithuania Act, Article 24(1); Netherlands Act, Article 13; Philippines Act, Article 8.1; Poland Act, Articles 7 and 36; Portugal Act, Article 14(1); Russia Act, Section 19(1); Singapore Model Code, Principle 7, Section 4.7.1; Slovakia Act, Section 15(1); Spain Act, Article 9; United Arab Emirates Act, Articles 15(1) and 16(1); and UK Act, Schedule 1, Part I, Seventh Principle.

The term "information security" means protecting information and information systems from unauthorized access, use, disclosure, disruption, modification, or destruction in order to provide — (A) integrity, which means guarding against improper information modification or destruction, and includes ensuring information nonrepudiation and authenticity; (B) confidentiality, which means preserving authorized restrictions on access and disclosure, including means for protecting personal privacy and proprietary information; and (C) availability, which means ensuring timely and reliable access to and use of information.[9]

Regardless of the approach taken in security statutes and regulations, the primary objectives of information security (and the laws that address it) are to:

- ensure the *confidentiality* of information;
- control *access* to systems, networks, and information;
- properly *authenticate* information and persons and devices seeking access to it;
- ensure the *integrity* of systems, networks, and information; and
- ensure the *availability* of systems, networks, and information.

Each of these objectives may be summarized as follows:

1.2.1 Confidentiality

Confidentiality is "the property that data or information is not made available or disclosed to unauthorized persons or processes."[10] It involves controlling access to information in order to prevent its disclosure to unauthorized

---

[9] FISMA, 44 USC § 3542(b)(1).
[10] HIPAA Security Regulations, 45 CFR Section 164.304.

individuals or systems. Thus, a loss of confidentiality is the unauthorized disclosure of information.

Ensuring confidentiality requires implementing processes, policies, and controls to protect information against unauthorized access or use.[11] It involves protecting information so that unauthorized persons cannot have access to it and, in some cases, protecting information so that even if unauthorized access is obtained, the information is unreadable (e.g. encrypted).

Two key requirements for ensuring the confidentiality of information are *access control* and *authentication*.

1.2.2 Access control

Access control involves determining "who" can access a system and the information it contains, and "what" they can do once they are granted access. It then requires implementation of security controls, such as user ID and password procedures, to implement and enforce those decisions.

The objective of access control is to ensure confidentiality – i.e. to allow access by authorized individuals and devices and to disallow access to all others. Thus, access control procedures should ensure that only persons or devices that are authorized to access a system are able to do so, and further, it should establish limits on that access so that they are able to access only those portions of the system and data directly relevant to their job or function.

---

[11] FFIEC, *IT Examinations Handbook – Information Security* (July 2006) p. 2.

Accordingly, access control has two basic dimensions. The first is determining whether a particular person (or device) is authorized to access the system or network generally. The second is determining whether such person (or device) is authorized to access specific data or functionalities within the system, and if so, what rights and privileges they have (e.g. to view the data, edit the data, delete the data, etc.).

Who (or what) is allowed access will, of course, vary depending upon the portion of the system and/or the information involved. Authorized individuals may be employees, service providers, vendors, contractors, customers, or visitors. Authorized devices may include processors, routers, or servers.

In all cases, however, access should be provided only to previously approved individuals and devices whose identity is properly verified (see discussion of *authentication* below), and their activities should be limited to the minimum required for business purposes.[12]

1.2.3 Authentication

Authentication is the process of determining whether someone or something is, in fact, who or what it is declared to be.[13] With individuals, for example, it includes the process of confirming the asserted identity of a person, in order to determine who is the source or origin of a communication, or who is trying to access the system.

---

[12] FFIEC, *IT Examination Handbook – Information Security* (July 2006) p. 22.
[13] See US Federal Rules of Evidence 901(a).

Typical legal definitions of authentication include: "the corroboration that a person is the one claimed,"[14] "utilizing digital credentials to assure the identity of users and validate their access,"[15] and a "procedure for checking a user's identity."[16]

With respect to *computer systems and networks*, authentication is used for access control – i.e. to determine who is trying to get in. It involves the process of verifying that someone trying to access the system (or particular data on the system) is who they claim to be when they log on. For example, when someone tries to access the Microsoft internal network claiming to be Bill Gates, Microsoft needs a method by which it can determine whether the person seeking access is, in fact, the person it has previously identified as Bill Gates and approved for access. Historically the most common means of authentication has been through the use of user names and passwords.

Note, however, that the process of authenticating a person is not the same as granting that person access rights to resources within the system. The latter is achieved through access control (described above). Once a person is reliably authenticated, access controls are designed to control what rights and privileges are granted to such person by the system (e.g. what information the person is authorized to access on the system, and whether such access is "view only" or whether it also includes the right alter and/or delete such information). Thus, for example, now that Bill Gates is no longer a day-to-day participant in the operation of Microsoft, he may still have the right to access the

---

[14] HIPAA Security Regulations, 45 CFR Section 164.304.
[15] Homeland Security Act of 2002 § 1001(b), amending 44 USC § 3532(b)(1)(D).
[16] Spain Royal Decree 1720/2007, Article 5(2)(b).

company's internal network, but he may not be authorized to see the personnel files of its employees.

With respect to *electronic communications*, authentication involves assuring both parties to the transaction that the other person (or entity or device) is who he or she (or it) claims to be. This allows the recipient to verify who originated a communication. A party entering into an online transaction in reliance of an electronic message must be confident of the source of that message. For example, when a bank receives an electronic payment order from a customer directing that money be paid to a third party, the bank must be able to verify the source of the request and ensure that it is not dealing with an impostor.

With respect to *electronic records*, authentication involves verifying that the author, or sender, is who they claim to be, and in some cases, ensuring that such person has approved, consented to, or otherwise adopted (e.g. signed) the contents of the record. A party must be able to establish the authenticity of its electronic transactions should a dispute arise. For example, if one party to an electronic contract later disavows any involvement, the other party may need to prove the first party's approval of the contract to a court. A court, however, will first require that the party establish authenticity of the record that the party retained of that communication before the court will consider it as evidence.[17]

In all cases, note that there is a difference between identification and authentication. *Identification* is the

---

[17] See e.g. *US v. Eisenberg*, 807 F.2d 1446 (8th Cir. 1986) (disputing the authenticity of letter); *US v. Grande*, 620 F.2d 1026 (4th Cir. 1980) (disputing authenticity of invoice), *cert. denied*, 449 US 830, 919 (1980).

process of verifying a person's identity (such as during an account origination process). *Authentication* is the process of confirming that a person presenting him or herself as a previously identified person is, in fact, that person (such as when a person attempts to gain access to an online system). In other words, authentication is the act of verifying a claim of identity.

For example, a bank might identify a person opening a bank account as Bill Gates of Microsoft. The bank might do this by examining his driver's license, doing a credit check, and checking with some references in order to determine that this is a person it would like to do business with (identification). Someone might later go into the bank to make a withdrawal, and tell the bank teller he is Bill Gates (a claim of identity). To verify his claim of identity, the bank teller might ask to see a government-issued photo ID, such as his driver's license. If the name, address, and photo on the ID document match the name and address of the account involved, and the photo matches the person standing in front of the teller, the teller has authenticated that Bill Gates is who he claims to be.

Existing methods for authenticating an individual, who has previously been identified, involve one or more of three basic "*factors*":

- something the person *knows* (e.g. a PIN, password or mother's maiden name);[18]

---

[18] The use of a user name or ID, coupled with a secret string of characters such as a password or PIN, is one of the most common authentication methods. User IDs combined with passwords or PINS are considered a single factor authentication technique. The security provided by user IDs and passwords is, of course, dependent upon the password being kept a secret.

- something the person *possesses* (e.g. an ATM card, a smart card, driver's license, or other physical token);[19]
- something the person *is* (e.g. a biometric characteristic,[20] such as a fingerprint or retinal pattern).

Thus, for example, the online use of a user ID and password is *single factor authentication* (i.e. something the user knows); whereas, a transaction using an ATM typically requires *two factor authentication*: something the user possesses (i.e. the ATM card) combined with something the user knows (i.e. the PIN number).[21] Authentication methods that depend on more than one factor typically are more difficult to compromise than single factor systems. Accordingly, properly designed and implemented multi-factor authentication methods are more reliable methods of authentication and stronger fraud deterrents.

1.2.4 Integrity

Integrity relates to reliability. Typical legal definitions include: "the property that data or information have not

---

[19] Tokens are physical devices designed for use in authentication systems and/or to hold authenticating information. These include smart cards, and ATM cards. The use of a token represents authentication using "something the customer possesses," and is typically part of a two factor authentication process, complemented by a password as the other factor.

[20] A biometric identifier measures an individual's unique physical characteristic or behavior and compares it to a stored digital template to authenticate the individual. Thus, it represents "something the user is". Commonly used biometrics include a person's voice, fingerprint, hand or face geometry, the iris or retina in an eye, or the way the person signs a document or enters key board strokes. The security of a biometric identifier rests on the ability of the digitally stored characteristic to relate to only one individual in a defined population.

[21] FFIEC, *Authentication in an Internet Banking Environment*, 12 October 2005 (FFIEC Guidance), available at www.ffiec.gov/pdf/authentication_guidance.pdf, p. 3.

been altered or destroyed in an unauthorized manner,"[22] and "guarding against improper information modification or destruction, [including] ensuring information nonrepudiation and authenticity."[23] A loss of integrity is the unauthorized modification or destruction of information.

The objective of integrity can be viewed from two perspectives: system integrity (i.e. the integrity of the computers, network, and software that comprise the system), and data integrity. Both relate to the processes, policies, and controls used to ensure information has not been altered in an unauthorized manner and that systems are free from unauthorized manipulation that will compromise accuracy, completeness, and reliability.[24]

System integrity is concerned with ensuring that the computer system and network operate properly, are correctly configured, and that no changes are made except as authorized. *Data integrity* is concerned with the accuracy and completeness of information, and with ensuring that no unauthorized alterations are made to such data, either intentionally or accidentally.

1.2.5 Availability

Availability refers to the ability to access and use information. Typical legal definitions include: "the property that data or information is accessible and useable

---

[22] HIPAA Security Regulations, 45 CFR Section 164.304.
[23] US Homeland Security Act of 2002, 44 USC § 3532(b)(1)(A); FISMA, 44 USC Section 3542(b)(1).
[24] FFIEC, *IT Examinations Handbook – Information Security* (July 2006) p. 2.

upon demand by an authorized person,"[25] and "ensuring timely and reliable access to and use of information."[26] A loss of availability is the disruption of access to or use of information or an information system.

The objective of availability involves ensuring that the computer systems, networks, and data are operational, fully functioning, available for use, and accessible whenever needed. This means that the computing system used to store and process information, the security controls used to protect it, and the communication channels used to access it must be functioning correctly and must be able to withstand a variety of possible disruptive events, such as power failures, natural disasters, accidents, or attacks.

The goal is to ensure authorized users have prompt access to information. The objective of availability protects against intentional or accidental attempts to deny legitimate users access to information or systems.[27] Today, for most businesses, if their computer system is unavailable, the business is seriously affected.

1.3 Threats addressed by information security

Threats to the security of information systems and data are typically divided into three categories: physical and environmental threats, technical threats, and people threats. Moreover, within each category it is important to distinguish between unintentional events (ranging from unavoidable acts of nature to possibly avoidable mistakes

---

[25] HIPAA Security Regulations, 45 CFR Section 164.304.
[26] US Homeland Security Act of 2002, 44 USC 3532(b)(1); FISMA, 44 USC Section 3542(b)(1).
[27] FFIEC, *IT Examinations Handbook – Information Security* (July 2006) p. 2.

by people) and intentional attacks, both by insiders and outsiders.

Physical and environmental threats: involve the theft, damage, destruction or other interference with the operation of the physical elements comprising the information system (e.g. servers, laptop computers, storage media, etc.). They include: (1) natural disasters or so-called acts of God, such as earthquakes, hurricanes, floods, storms, tornadoes, fire, and lightning that physically damage information systems or interfere with their operation; (2) infrastructure failures that cause problems, such as power failures or fluctuations, hardware failures, water damage, and improper air conditioning, humidity, or heating; and (3) intentional acts aimed at the physical computer system, such as theft of equipment or storage media, criminal destruction, such as vandalism or sabotage, as well as civil disorders, terrorism, and war.

Technical threats: are those carried out by the use of computer code or other automated mechanisms. Such threats do not damage the physical equipment, but may result in the inoperability or improper operation of a computer system or network, the unauthorized disclosure, alteration, or destruction of information, or other similar inappropriate or destructive results. Although frequently the result of human programming activity, technical threats can be unintentional or negligent, as well as intentional and malicious.

- Unintentional or negligent technical threats include software bugs that occur during the programming of a computer system, and system configuration errors, such as the use of improper settings or parameters when software is installed.

- Intentional and malicious technical threats, on the other hand, typically involve the use of computer code or other technical devices designed to cause trouble. This includes, for example, software bugs intentionally added to computer programs, malicious software that modifies or destroys data (or engages in other mischief), such as viruses, worms, Trojan horses, spyware programs designed to copy and transmit communications or other information, network spoofing, denial of service attacks, password cracking, e-mail hijacking, packet replay, and packet modification.

People threats: come from individuals, sometimes in the form of direct action and other times from individuals who implement some of the technical threats discussed above. Although press coverage of security breaches is focused primarily on outsiders (such as hackers) who break into an organization's computer system, more often than not the primary people threats come from insiders (such as employees, consultants, or others that are authorized to have access to the system).

In some cases, for example, individuals simply abuse their authorization (e.g. when an employee who has access to customer credit card information sells some of that information to a third party). In other cases, however, insider-originated security breaches are the result of simple negligence, inattention, or lack of education (e.g. when an employee who does not understand proper procedures inadvertently discloses confidential information). Unintentional mistakes or omissions by employees who are not properly trained or who are negligent, such as system administrator errors, operator errors, and programming errors are common.

Outsiders are often able to breach an organization's security through a variety of means. These include impersonation (e.g. misrepresenting the identity or source), social engineering (e.g. talking an unsuspecting insider into releasing password information or otherwise allowing access or disclosing confidential information), hacking (gaining access through the use of technical tools, such as exploiting weaknesses in software systems), or brute force attacks (e.g. guessing passwords until one is successful).

1.4 Information security controls

Security controls (sometimes called security measures or safeguards) are the various policies, procedures, organizational structures, devices, hardware, software, and other means used to protect information and systems from the many threats they face. For purposes of classification, they can be viewed from two different but overlapping perspectives: by the *type* of security control and by the *category* of security control.

1.4.1 Types of security control

Security controls designed to protect information from threats can generally be grouped into three types (or levels) as follows:

- *Preventative security controls* are designed to defend against threats and prevent the occurrence of events that compromise security.[28] An example of a preventative security measure is a lock on a door (to prevent access to

---

[28] See e.g. FISMA, 44 USC Section 3544(b)(2).

a room), or a firewall (to prevent unwanted remote access to a computer system);

- *Detective security controls* are designed to identify security breaches and other threats after they have occurred.[29] An example of a detective security measure is a smoke alarm (which is designed to detect a fire), or intrusion detection software (which is designed to track unauthorized access to a computer system);

- *Reactive security controls* are designed to respond to a security breach, and typically include efforts to stop or contain the breach, identify the party or parties involved, and allow recovery of information that is lost or damaged.[30] An example of reactive security is calling the police after an alarm detects that a burglary is in process, or shutting down a computer system after intrusion detection software determines that an unauthorized user has obtained access to the system.

Security laws and regulations often refer to these three types of security control. The HIPAA Security Regulations, for example, require regulated entities to "implement policies and procedures to prevent, detect, contain, and correct security violations."[31]

1.4.2 Categories of security control

Security controls designed to protect information from threats are also generally grouped into three separate categories: physical security controls, technical security

---

[29] See e.g. FISMA, 44 USC Section 3544(b)(7).
[30] See e.g. FISMA, 44 USC Section 3544(b)(7).
[31] HIPAA Security Regulations, 45 CFR Section 164.308(a)(1)(i).

controls, and administrative (or organizational) security controls. Most statutes and regulations reference these three categories. For example, regulations often require companies to "implement a comprehensive written information security program that includes administrative, technical, and physical safeguards,"[32] to "maintain reasonable and appropriate administrative, technical, and physical safeguards . . . ,"[33] or to "implement appropriate technical and organizational measures."[34]

Security controls adopted within each of these categories should include the three types (or levels) of security measures noted above. The following sub-sections will describe each of the three categories of security and provide examples of each type (or level) of security measure that might be used within each category.

Physical security controls:[35] are designed to protect the tangible items that comprise the physical computer system and network and that store the data, including servers, terminals that have access to the system, storage devices, and the like. They involve monitoring and controlling the environment of the work place and computing facilities where the computer hardware and storage media are located. They are intended to prevent unauthorized persons from entering that environment,[36] as well as to help protect against natural disasters. One regulation defines physical safeguards as "physical measures, policies, and procedures

---

[32] GLB Security Regulations, 12 CFR Part 30, Appendix B, Section II.A.
[33] HIPAA, 42 USC Section 1320d-2(d)(2).
[34] EU Data Protection Directive, Article 17(1).
[35] See e.g. HIPAA Security Regulations, 45 CFR Section 164.304.
[36] Physical security includes "tangible means of preventing unauthorized physical access to a system. E.g. fences, walls, and other barriers; locks, safes, and vaults; dogs and armed guards; sensors and alarm bells." Internet RFC 2828.

to protect a covered entity's electronic information systems and related buildings and equipment, from natural and environmental hazards, and unauthorized intrusion."[37]

Examples of preventive physical security controls designed to keep out inappropriate persons include locks, fences, security guards, double door systems, and key card access controls. Examples of detective physical security controls designed to warn of a security breach or environmental hazard include sensors and alarms such as motion detectors, smoke and fire detectors, and closed circuit television monitors. Reactive physical security measures intended to respond to security events include sprinkler systems, locking doors, and systems designed to automatically notify the police and fire departments of a problem.

Technical security controls:[38] (also called logical controls) typically involve the use of software and data safeguards incorporated into computer hardware, software, and related devices. They are designed to ensure system availability, provide access control, authenticate persons seeking access, protect the integrity of information communicated and stored on the system, and ensure confidentiality where appropriate.

Examples of preventive technical security controls designed to thwart hackers and malware include firewalls,[39] access control software, anti-virus software, passwords, PIN numbers, smart cards, biometric tokens, and encryption. Examples of detective technical security controls designed

---

[37] HIPAA Security Regulations, 45 CFR Section 164.304.
[38] See e.g. HIPAA Security Regulations, 45 CFR Section 164.312.
[39] A firewall is software that provides a barrier between an internal network and an external network, like the Internet. Firewalls control all incoming and outgoing communications.

to warn when a hacker has been successful include intrusion detection systems and audit trails. Reactive technical security measures intended to respond to security events might include cutting off access or taking a system down.

Administrative security controls:[40] (sometimes referred to as organizational security measures[41] or procedural controls), consist of written policies, procedures, standards and guidelines to ensure that only honest and qualified people are granted access, and their behavior is controlled to prevent unauthorized access and generally provide an acceptable level of protection for computing resources and data.[42] Administrative security measures also inform people how day-to-day operations are to be conducted.

Examples of preventive administrative controls include procedures for proper screening of personnel before hiring, security awareness education and training for employees, separation of duties so that no one employee can effectively compromise the system, procedures for employee termination, and requirements for appropriate supervision. Examples of detective administrative controls include regular employee security reviews and audits, employee reporting, and rotation of duties. Reactive administrative security measures include appropriate discipline for employees who violate policies.

---

[40] See e.g. HIPAA Security Regulations, 45 CFR Section 164.308.
[41] See e.g. GLB Security Regulations, 12 CFR Part 30 Appendix B, Part II.A; EU Data Protection Directive, Article 17(1).
[42] RFC 2828, available at http://www.faqs.org/rfcs/rfc2828.html. See also, HIPAA regulations, 45 CFR 164.304.

1: Security Basics: The Legal Perspective

Most security statutes and regulations require physical, technical, and administrative (or organizational) security measures, either expressly or impliedly.

CHAPTER 2: LEGAL RESPONSE TO SECURITY

Understanding corporate obligations to address data security begins with a high level understanding of the legal response to security threats.

The law essentially takes a two-pronged approach to addressing the challenges posed by the extensive use of electronic information, and the potential damages that can arise when security is breached and information is compromised. First, the law declares illegal certain conduct that breaches the security of one's data, and provides punishment for those who engage in such conduct. Second, the law imposes on those businesses that possess data an obligation to protect that data and the corresponding information systems in order to protect the various stakeholders.

2.1 Declaring conduct illegal

Many countries, and all states within the US, have now enacted some form of cybercrime legislation designed to deter and punish activities that threaten the security of computer systems or the information they contain. Some jurisdictions have enacted comprehensive computer crime statutes, while others have simply modified existing criminal statutes to better fit computer crimes. In both cases, the statutes were enacted in response to an escalation in computer crime and the perceived inability of traditional criminal statutes to cover all possible computer-related crimes.

For example, the Preamble to the Council of Europe Convention on Cybercrime[1] makes note of:

- the need to pursue, as a matter of priority, a common criminal policy aimed at the protection of society against cybercrime;
- the profound changes brought about by the digitalization, convergence and continuing globalization of computer networks;
- the risk that computer networks and electronic information may also be used for committing criminal offences and that evidence relating to such offences may be stored and transferred by these networks; and
- the need to deter action directed against the confidentiality, integrity and availability of computer systems, networks and computer data as well as the misuse of such systems, networks and data.

Likewise, in the statement of legislative intent in the Florida computer crime statute[2] the legislature "finds and declares" that "Computer-related crime is a growing problem in government as well as in the private sector," and that "While various forms of computer crime might possibly be the subject of criminal charges based on other provisions of law, it is appropriate and desirable that a supplemental and additional statute be provided which proscribes various forms of computer abuse."

To address these needs, cybercrime statutes typically seek to protect the security of corporate data by outlawing offenses

---

[1] Council of Europe, Convention on Cybercrime – Budapest, 23.XI.2001 (ETS No. 185) (2002) (hereinafter "Cybercrime Convention"),
http://conventions.coe.int/Treaty/EN/Treaties/Html/185.htm.
[2] Fla. Stat. Ann. § 815.02.

against the confidentiality, integrity, and availability of computer systems, networks, and data,[3] such as:

- unauthorized access to data;
- unauthorized use of data;
- unauthorized interception of data;
- unauthorized suppression, alteration, deterioration, or destruction of data;
- interference with the operation of a system;
- misuse of devices;
- denial of access;
- unauthorized possession/use of passwords.

By better defining the types of online activities that are prohibited, these statutes have greatly assisted prosecutors in filing charges for computer-related crimes and have freed them from having to stretch existing laws to fit offenses for which they were not designed.

Virtually every cybercrime statute prohibits unauthorized access to or use of a computer or its data. Examples include the US Computer Fraud and Abuse Act,[4] the computer crime statutes enacted in each US state,[5] the Council of Europe Cybercrime Convention,[6] and the cybercrime laws in many countries.[7] Likewise, these

---

[3] Cybercrime statutes also address other computer-based crimes, such as: (1) offenses involving use of the computer, network, or data as a tool for committing another crime (such as computer-related forgery, computer-related fraud or using a computer to commit other crimes, and identity theft); (2) offenses involving content, such as child pornography; (3) offenses related to the infringement of rights (such as copyright infringement, identity theft, defamation, and spam); and (4) theft of computer services. See e.g. Cybercrime Convention.
[4] 18 USC Section 1030(a).
[5] A list is available at www.crime-research.org/library/State.pdf.
[6] Cybercrime Convention, Article 2.
[7] See e.g. Australia Cybercrime Act of 2001, Section 478; Belgium Criminal Code, Section 550(b); Criminal Law of the People's Republic of China, Section 285-287.

statutes also make criminal the unauthorized alteration or destruction of data on the computer of another.[8]

Many cybercrime laws also prohibit a third party from intercepting electronic communications just as wiretapping laws prohibit the interception of telephone calls. In the US, for example, the Electronic Communications Privacy Act[9] prohibits both the unauthorized interception or disclosure of electronic communications in transit, as well as unauthorized access to, and disclosure of, stored electronic communications, including both voice mail and electronic mail.[10] Similarly, the Council of Europe Cybercrime Convention requires signatory countries to implement domestic legislation that makes criminal the unauthorized interception of non-public transmissions of computer data to, from, or within a computer system.[11]

Denial of access, or other means of interfering with the legitimate access of someone authorized to use a computer system or database is also prohibited. Many of the US state computer crime statutes, for example, make it a felony to "willfully, knowingly, and without authorization den[y] or cause the denial of computer services to an authorized user of such computer system services. . . ."[12]

Some cybercrime statutes also prohibit intentional attempts to identify valid access codes without authorization[13] or to take or steal passwords.[14] Other statutes focus on

---

[8] See e.g. Cybercrime Convention, Article 4.
[9] 18 USC § 2510 *et seq.*
[10] 18 USC §§ 2701, 2702.
[11] Cybercrime Convention, Article 3.
[12] See e.g. Fla. Stats. Ann. § 815.06. See also Cybercrime Convention Article 5.
[13] See e.g. Md. Crimes and Punishments Code Ann. § 146.
[14] See e.g. Mo. Ann. State § 569.095.

prohibiting one person from providing another with the means or the information needed to illegally access a computer.

A law in the state of Georgia, for example, provides that:

> ...[a]ny person who discloses a number, code, password, or other means of access to a computer or computer network knowing that such disclosure is without authority and which results in damages (including the fair market value of any services used and victim expenditure) to the owner of the computer or computer network in excess of $500 shall be guilty of the crime of computer password disclosure. [15]

It is also a federal crime under the Computer Fraud and Abuse Act to knowingly, and with intent to defraud, traffic any password through which a computer may be accessed without authorization if such trafficking affects interstate or foreign commerce, or if the computer is used by or for the US government. [16]

2.2 Requiring the protection of data

The second prong of the legal approach to security is to require those who own or possess sensitive data to take appropriate measures to protect both: (1) the data itself, and (2) the persons who might be affected by a breach of the security of that data. This approach is based on a recognition that companies which possess valuable data, the compromise of which affects many corporate stakeholders, bear some responsibility to those stakeholders for its protection. Moreover, due to the nature of electronic data, whereby it can be stolen or altered without detection, and

---

[15] Ga. Code Ann. § 16-9-93(e).
[16] 18 USC § 1030(a)(6).

the crime can be committed remotely by someone in another jurisdiction who most often cannot even be identified, much less prosecuted, it reflects the reality that the security measures adopted by the data owner may be the only viable way to address the problem of breach.

The legal obligations of a business to protect the security of its own data, and to help mitigate any losses that third parties may suffer in the event of a data breach, is the subject of this book. In particular, this book will focus on three key aspects of those legal obligations:

- The obligation to provide security for corporate data generally;
- The legal standard by which that general obligation is measured; and
- The duty to warn individuals of the breach of their information.

CHAPTER 3: THE GENERAL DUTY TO PROVIDE SECURITY

3.1 The basic obligation

The obligation to provide security for corporate data is, in essence, a duty to provide "reasonable" or "appropriate" physical, technical, and administrative security measures to ensure the confidentiality, integrity, and availability of corporate data.

The meaning of that obligation, and its various requirements, will be explored in Chapters 4, 5, and 6. This chapter will examine where the obligation comes from, which companies it applies to, what types of data are covered by the obligation, and who in the company is responsible for legal compliance.

3.2 Where does the obligation come from?

There is no single law, statute, or regulation that governs a company's obligations to provide security for its information. Corporate legal obligations to implement security measures are set forth in an ever-expanding patchwork of state, federal, and international laws, regulations, and enforcement actions, as well as common law duties, contractual commitments, and other expressed and implied obligations to provide "reasonable" or "appropriate" security for corporate data.

Some laws seek to protect the company and its shareholders, investors, and business partners. Others focus on the interests of individual employees, customers, and third parties. And in other cases, governmental regulatory interests, or evidentiary requirements are at stake. Many of the requirements are industry-specific (e.g. focused on the financial industry or the healthcare industry) or data-specific (e.g. focused on personal information or financial data). Others focus only on public companies. When viewed as a group, however, laws and regulations addressing security provide ever-expanding coverage of most corporate activity.

The most common sources of legal obligations on a business to provide security for its own data include the following:[1]

Statutes and regulations: Numerous statutes and regulations impose obligations to provide security. Sometimes they are readily recognized by their use of terms such as "security" or "safeguards,"[2] but in many cases the fact that they impose security obligations is evident only by their use of language relating to the objectives of security, such as "authenticate," "integrity," "confidentiality," "availability of data," and the like.[3]

Some of the most common sources of statutes and regulations with security requirements include:

• Privacy laws and regulations that require companies to implement information security measures to protect certain personal data they maintain about individuals;

---

[1] See Appendix for a compilation of some of the key laws and regulations governing information security.
[2] See e.g. EU Data Protection Directive and HIPAA, cited in Appendix.
[3] See e.g. E-SIGN, UETA, and UN Electronic Communications Convention cited in Appendix.

- Electronic transaction laws designed to ensure the enforceability of electronic documents generally;

- Corporate governance legislation and regulations designed to protect public companies and their shareholders, investors, and business partners;

- Unfair business practice laws and related government enforcement actions; and

- Sector-specific regulations imposing security obligations with respect to specific data.

A list of some of the more common statutes and regulations governing the security of personal data (particularly in the US) is set forth in the Appendix.

Common law obligations: For years, commentators have argued that there exists a common law duty to provide appropriate security for corporate data.[4] Courts in the US are now beginning to accept that view, and recent decisions have recognized that there may be a common law duty to provide security, the breach of which constitutes a tort.[5] *See cases cited in Appendix and discussed in Section 3.3.*

---

[4] See e.g. Kimberly Kiefer and Randy V. Sabett, *Openness of Internet Creates Potential for Corporate Information Security Liability*, BNA Privacy & Security Law Report, Vol. 1, No. 25, at 788 (24 June 2002); Alan Charles Raul, Frank R. Volpe, and Gabriel S. Meyer, *Liability for Computer Glitches and Online Security Lapses*, BNA Electronic Commerce Law Report, Vol. 6, No. 31 at 849 (8 August 2001); Erin Kenneally, *The Byte Stops Here: Duty and Liability for Negligent Internet Security*, Computer Security Journal, Vol. XVI, No. 2, 2000.

[5] See e.g. *Wolfe v. MBNA America Bank*, 485 F.Supp.2d 874, 882 (W.D. Tenn. 2007); *Guin v. Brazos Higher Education Service*, Civ. No. 05-668, 2006 US Dist. Lexis 4846 (D. Minn. 7 February 2006); and *Bell v. Michigan Council*, 2005 Mich. App. Lexis 353 (Mich. App. 15 February 2005) (all affirming a negligence cause of action). See also, *In Re TJX Companies Retail Security Breach Litigation*, 2007 US Dist. Lexis 77236 (D. Mass. 12 October 2007) (rejecting a negligence claim due to the economic loss doctrine, but allowing a negligent misrepresentation claim to proceed).

Rules of evidence: Recent court decisions, at least at the federal level in the US, suggest that security will increasingly be a requirement for the admissibility of digital records.[6] *See discussion in Section 3.4.3.*

Industry standards imposed by contract: In some cases, companies become contractually obligated to comply with the requirements of certain technical security standards. Examples include the Payment Card Industry Data Security Standard (PCI Standard)[7] that merchants must agree to as a condition of accepting credit cards, the EV SSL Certificate Guidelines[8] that certification authorities must agree to in order to issue EV SSL certificates, and the international ISO27001 standard[9] sometimes imposed upon businesses by contract with trading partners. In each of these cases, the standard has no legal authority by itself, but becomes binding typically through a contractual agreement. In some cases, however, such as in Japan, compliance with a particular standard (in that case, ISO27001) may be required by regulation.

System rules imposed by contract: In some cases, a company may be subject to certain system rules that impose security obligations on it. This generally occurs, for example, in connection with use of various electronic payment systems (such as the ACH payment system in the US)[10] or federated identity systems that require agreement

---

[6] See e.g. *American Express v. Vinhnee*, 2005 Bankr. Lexis 2602 (9th Cir. Bk. App. Panel, 2005); *Lorraine v. Markel*, 2007 US Dist. Lexis 33020 (D. MD. 4 May 2007).
[7] Available at www.pcisecuritystandards.org.
[8] Available at www.cabforum.org.
[9] ISO/IEC 27001, *Information Technology – Security Techniques – Information Security Management Systems – Requirements* (Oct. 2005) (hereinafter "ISO27001"), available for purchase at http://www.itgovernance.co.uk/standards.aspx.
[10] See e.g. National Automated Clearing House Association, *2008 ACH Rules*.

to system rules as a condition of participation (such as EV SSL Certificates).[11]

Other contractual obligations: As businesses increasingly become aware of the need to protect the security of their own data, they frequently try to satisfy their obligation (at least in part) by contract in those situations where third parties will have possession of, or access to, such business data. This is particularly common, for example, in outsourcing agreements where a company's data will be processed by a third party. In such cases, laws and regulations such as the EU Data Protection Directive and US GLB Security Regulations typically require that businesses impose appropriate security obligations on outsource providers they use to process their data (*see Section 5.6*). In addition, in any situation where a business may have access to someone else's data, it is quite common for the other party to impose both confidentiality and security obligations with respect to that data.

Self-imposed obligations: In many cases, companies impose security obligations on themselves. Through statements in privacy policies, on websites, or in advertising materials, for example, companies often make representations regarding the level of security they provide for their data (particularly the personal data they collect from the persons to whom the statements are made). By making such statements, companies impose on themselves an obligation to comply with the standard they have represented to the public that they meet. If those statements are not true, or if they are misleading, such statements may

---

[11]See CA/Browser Forum, *EV SSL Certificate Guidelines*, available at www.cabforum.org.

become, in effect, deceptive trade practices. Through a series of enforcement actions in the US, for example, both the FTC and several state Attorneys General have used applicable deceptive business practice statutes[12] to bring enforcement actions against the offending companies (*see Section 3.3*).

The bottom line is that a company's duty to provide security may come from several different sources and several different jurisdictions – each perhaps regulating a different aspect of corporate information – but the net result (and certainly the trend) is a general obligation to provide security for all corporate data and information systems. In other words, information security is no longer just good business practice. It is a legal obligation.

3.3 Who does the obligation apply to?

Viewing security statutes and regulations as a group, it is clear that the legal obligation to provide security for corporate data generally applies to all companies in all industry sectors. Some individual statutes and regulations may be limited to certain industry sectors, but it is likely that all companies are subject to the obligation from a variety of the sources noted above.

In Europe, the legal duty to provide security generally applies to all companies that possess personal information. In fact, the obligation to provide security for the protection of personal information is one of the key principles set forth

---

[12] See e.g. Section 5 of the US FTC Act, 15 USC 45(a)(1), and equivalent state laws.

in the EU Data Protection Directive.[13] The Directive establishes omnibus protection for the privacy of all personal information of EU residents, and applies to all companies established in the EU, that make use of equipment within the EU, or that are in another jurisdiction where an EU member country's law applies by virtue of private international law.

Each of the various EU country implementations of the Directive also impose such a requirement for security on all companies.[14] Outside of the EU numerous other country privacy laws also impose a general duty on all companies to protect the security of personal information. Examples include Canada, Japan, Argentina, South Korea, Hong Kong, and Australia.[15]

In the US, obligations to provide security were initially applied on a sector-specific basis. The first substantive corporate obligations to provide security for personal information appeared in the Health Insurance Portability and Accountability Act of 1996 (HIPAA),[16] which regulated the healthcare sector. This was followed in 1999 by the Gramm-Leach-Bliley Act (GLB Act),[17] which regulated the financial sector. Detailed security regulations implementing the security provision of GLB (the GLB

---

[13] Directive 95/46/EC of the European Parliament and of the Council of 24 October 1995 on the protection of individuals with regard to the processing of personal data and on the free movement of such data (hereinafter "EU Data Protection Directive").

[14] See statutes listed in Appendix.

[15] See statutes listed in Appendix.

[16] Health Insurance Portability and Accountability Act of 1996 (HIPAA), 42 USC 1320d-2 and 1320d-4.

[17] Gramm-Leach-Bliley Financial Services Modernization Act (GLB), Pub. L. No. 106-102, 113 Stat. 1338 (12 November 1999), at §§ 501 and 505(b), 15 USC §§ 6801, 6805.

Security Regulations) were released in 2001[18] and security regulations implementing the security provision under HIPAA (the HIPAA Security Regulations) were released in 2003.[19]

Since then, however, the sector-specific approach to imposing security obligations to protect personal information has significantly shifted. Today, US law is rapidly expanding to impose security requirements on all companies (regardless of sector), thereby matching the EU approach, at least with regard to the security of personal information.[20] This is occurring in three ways:

First, through a series of enforcement actions and consent decrees beginning in 2002, both the FTC and several state attorneys general have, in effect, extended security obligations regarding personal information to non-regulated industries by virtue of Section 5 of the FTC Act and similar state laws. Initially, cases were based on the alleged failure of companies to provide adequate information security contrary to representations they made to customers.[21] In other words, these were claims of deceptive trade practices. But beginning in June 2005, the FTC significantly

---

[18] See Gramm-Leach-Bliley Act (GLB), Public Law 106-102, §§ 501 and 505(b), 15 USC §§ 6801, 6805, and GLB Security Regulations at 12 CFR Part 30, Appendix B (OCC), 12 CFR Part 208, Appendix D (Federal Reserve System), 12 CFR Part 364, Appendix B (FDIC), 12 CFR Part 568 (Office of Thrift Supervision) and 16 CFR Part 314 (FTC).

[19] HIPAA Security Regulations, 45 CFR Part 164.

[20] There have also been efforts in the US to pursue comprehensive federal privacy similar to the approach taken by many other countries. See e.g. Microsoft position paper at www.microsoft.com/presspass/download/features/2005/PrivacyLegislationCallWP.doc. While it remains to be seen whether that approach will ultimately be adopted, it is clear that the combination of US state and federal has, in effect, imposed a comprehensive obligation of security with respect to all personal information held by all companies.

[21] See e.g. FTC enforcement actions regarding *In the matter of Sunbelt Lending Services, Inc.*; *In the matter of Petco Animal Supplies, Inc.*; *In the matter of MTS, Inc. d/b/a Tower records/Books/Video*; In the matter of Guess? Inc.; *FTC V. Microsoft*; and *In the matter of Eli Lilly and Company* cited in the Appendix.

broadened the scope of its enforcement actions by asserting that a failure to provide appropriate information security for consumer personal information was, itself, an unfair trade practice – even in the absence of any false representations by the defendant as to the state of its security.[22]

Second, several states have enacted laws imposing a general obligation on all companies to ensure the security of personal information. The first was California, which enacted legislation in 2004 requiring all businesses to "implement and maintain reasonable security procedures and practices" to protect personal information about California residents from unauthorized access, destruction, use, modification, or disclosure. Other states have recently followed suit, including Arkansas, Connecticut, Maryland, Massachusetts, Nevada, Oregon, Rhode Island, Texas, and Utah.[23]

Third, courts are also beginning to recognize that all companies have a common law duty to provide security for personal information, the breach of which constitutes a tort. In *Bell v. Michigan Council*, for example, the court held that "defendant did owe plaintiffs a duty to protect them from identity theft by providing some safeguards to ensure the security of their most essential confidential identifying information."[24] In *Guin v. Brazos Education*, the court acknowledged that in some negligence cases, a duty of care

---

[22] See e.g. FTC enforcement actions regarding *In the Matter of CardSystems Solutions, Inc.; United States v. ChoicePoint, Inc.; In the Matter of DSW Inc.; and In the Matter of BJ's Wholesale Club, Inc.* cited in the Appendix.
[23] See list in Appendix.
[24] *Bell v. Michigan Council*, 2005 Mich. App. Lexis 353 at *16 (Mich. App. 15 February 2005).

may be established by statute (in that case, the GLB Act).[25] And in *Wolfe v. MBNA America Bank*, the court found that where the injury is foreseeable and preventable, the "defendant has a duty to verify the authenticity and accuracy of a credit account application."[26]

In the case of *In Re TJX Companies Retail Security Breach Litigation*,[27] the court allowed plaintiffs to proceed on a "negligent misrepresentation" claim based on the theory that TJX and its acquiring bank made implied representations to the issuing banks that they took the security measures required by industry practice to safeguard personal and financial information. According to the court, the theory is that "TJX and [its acquiring bank] knew that the issuing banks were part of a financial network that relies on members taking appropriate security measures."[28]

3.4 What is covered?

The obligation to protect corporate information extends to most types of information. This includes, for example, financial information, personal information, tax-related records, employee information, transaction information, and trade secret and other confidential information. The obligation also applies regardless of the form of the information. Thus, for example, it includes databases, e-mails, text documents, spreadsheets, voicemail messages, pictures, video, and sound recordings.

---

[25] *Guin v. Brazos Higher Education Service*, Civ. No. 05-668, 2006 US Dist. Lexis 4846 at *9 (D. Minn. 7 February 2006).
[26] *Wolfe v. MBNA America Bank*, 485 F.Supp.2d 874, 882 (W.D. Tenn. 2007).
[27] *In Re TJX Companies Retail Security Breach Litigation*, 2007 US Dist. Lexis 77236 (D. Mass. 12 October 2007), pp. 28-29.
[28] Id.

Moreover, it is important to note that protecting information requires addressing the means by which such information is created, stored, and communicated. Thus, statutes and regulations governing information security often require the protection of the information systems and the data, messages, and information that is typically processed by, communicated via, and stored in, such information systems.

3.4.1 Personal data

Perhaps the biggest driver of laws requiring security is the concern for individual privacy. The obligation to provide adequate security for personal data collected, used, and/or maintained by a business is a fundamental component of all statements of basic privacy principles,[29] and a critical component of all privacy laws. The privacy of a person's data is illusory at best if there is no security for the data.

In Europe, the legal duty to provide security for the protection of personal information is one of the key principles set forth in the EU Data Protection Directive. It recognizes that the protection of the rights of data subjects, with respect to the processing of their personal data, requires the implementation of appropriate security

---

[29] See e.g. Australia, Information Privacy Principles under the Privacy Act 1988, Principle No. 4, available at www.privacy.gov.au/publications/ipps.html; AICPA and the Canadian Institute of Chartered Accountants (CICA), Generally Accepted Privacy principles, Principle No. 8, available at http://infotech.aicpa.org/Resources/Privacy/Generally+Accepted+Privacy+Principles; APEC, Privacy principles, Principle No. 7, available at http://austlii.edu.au/~graham/APEC/APECv10.doc; US-EU Safe Harbor Privacy Principles, available at www.export.gov/safeharbor/SHPRINCIPLESFINAL.htm; and Direct Marketing Association, Online Marketing Guidelines, available at www.the-dma.org/guidelines/onlineguidelines.shtml.

measures.[30]   Accordingly, the Directive requires EU Member States to enact legislation obligating the controllers of personal data to "implement appropriate technical and organizational measures to protect personal data against accidental or unlawful destruction or accidental loss, alteration, unauthorized disclosure or access, in particular where the processing involves the transmission of data over a network, and against all other unlawful forms of processing."[31]

Subsequent EU country implementations of the Directive all impose such a requirement to protect the security of personal information.[32]   Numerous other country privacy laws (which also tend to take an omnibus approach to privacy, like the EU) also impose a general duty on all companies to protect the security of personal information.[33]

Likewise, in the US, protecting personal information is the focus of numerous federal and state laws. These include sector-specific privacy laws such as the GLB Act (financial sector), HIPAA (healthcare sector), and the Privacy Act of 1974 (federal government), as well as numerous more general state laws, as outlined in the Appendix.

3.4.2 *Most other corporate data*

Although security obligations are often focused on personal data, other law, particularly in the US, is expanding such

---

[30] EU Data Protection Directive, Preamble at Para. 46.
[31] EU Data Protection Directive, Article 17(1).
[32] See statutes listed in Appendix.
[33] See e.g. the statutes in Canada, Japan, Argentina, South Korea, Hong Kong, and Australia listed in Appendix.

obligations to cover most other types of corporate data. This includes, for example:

- *Corporate financial data*: Corporate governance legislation and case law designed to protect the company and its shareholders, investors, and business partners, such as Sarbanes-Oxley and implementing regulations, require public companies to ensure that they have implemented appropriate information security controls with respect to their financial information.[34] Similarly, several SEC regulations impose a variety of requirements for internal controls over information systems.

- *Transaction records*: Electronic transaction laws designed to ensure the enforceability and compliance of electronic documents generally. Both the federal and state electronic transaction statutes (E-SIGN and UETA) require all companies to provide security for storage of electronic records relating to online transactions.

- *Tax records*: IRS regulations require companies to implement information security to protect electronic tax records, and as a condition to engaging in certain electronic transactions.

3.4.3 All digital records

Providing appropriate security to ensure the integrity of electronic records (and, where necessary, to authenticate the identity of the creator, sender, or signer of the record) will

---

[34] See generally, Bruce H. Nearon, Jon Stanley, Steven W. Teppler, and Joseph Burton, *Life after Sarbanes-Oxley: The Merger of Information Security and Accountability*, 45 Jurimetrics Journal 379-412 (2005).

likely be critical to courts when they are asked in a future dispute to admit electronic records into evidence. This conclusion is supported both by recent case law as well as provisions relating to the form requirement for an "original" in electronic transaction legislation.

Satisfying admissibility requirements: In the US, the federal appeals court decision in the case of *American Express v. Vinhnee*[35] suggests that appropriate security is a condition for the admissibility in evidence of electronic records. In that case, the court refused to admit electronic records into evidence because American Express did not adequately establish that they were "authentic." According to the court, the primary authenticity issue for admissibility is establishing "what has, or may have, happened to the record in the interval between when it was placed in the files and the time of trial." And to do this, the court said, "one must demonstrate that the record that has been retrieved from the file, be it paper or electronic, is the same as the record that was originally placed into the file."[36]

In other words, the court required evidence that appropriate security was in place to ensure the integrity of the electronic records from the time they were created until the time that they were introduced in court. As the court pointed out:

The logical questions extend beyond the identification of the particular computer equipment and programs used. The entity's policies and procedures for the use of the equipment, database, and programs are important. How access to the pertinent database is controlled and, separately, how access to the

---

[35] *American Express v. Vinhnee*, 336 B.R. 437; 2005 Bankr. Lexis 2602 (9th Cir. 16 December 2006).
[36] Id. p. 444.

specific program is controlled are important questions. How changes in the database are logged or recorded, as well as the structure and implementation of backup systems and audit procedures for assuring the continuing integrity of the database, are pertinent to the question of whether records have been changed since their creation.[37]

Thus, the court required a showing that "the business has developed a procedure for inserting data into the computer," and "the procedure must have built-in safeguards to ensure accuracy and identify errors." Those safeguards, the court noted, "subsume details regarding computer policy and system control procedures, including control of access to the database, control of access to the program, recording and logging of changes, backup practices, and audit procedures to assure the continuing integrity of the records."[38]

It remains to be seen whether, or to what extent, other courts will adopt this approach to admissibility of electronic evidence. Given the growing awareness of the ability to manipulate electronic data, however, it seems likely that this trend will only continue.

Satisfying requirements for an original: A similar issue arises regarding the way in which electronic transaction statutes generally treat the paper-based evidentiary requirement for an "original." Like the *Vinhnee* case, most major electronic transaction laws, such as E-SIGN,[39]

---

[37] Id. p. 445.
[38] Id. pp. 446-447.
[39] Electronic Signatures in Global and National Commerce Act (hereinafter "E-SIGN"), 15 USC 7001 *et seq.* E-SIGN is available at www.ntia.doc.gov/ntiahome/frnotices/2002/esign/report2003/ElectronicSignaturesAct.pdf

UETA,[40] the EU Electronic Signatures Directive,[41] and the 2005 United Nations Convention on the Use of Electronic Communications in International Contracts (UN Convention)[42] require assurances as to the integrity and accessibility of an electronic record as the condition required for treatment as an "original."

In the US, for example, to satisfy legal requirements that a record be presented or retained in original form, both E-SIGN and UETA require that the electronic record must "accurately reflect the information" and must "remain accessible" to all persons who are entitled to access.[43] To satisfy such requirements internationally, the UN Convention requires "a reliable assurance as to the integrity of the information" contained in an electronic communication, and that it must be "capable of being

---

[40] Uniform Electronic Transactions Act (hereinafter "UETA"), approved by the National Conference of Commissioners on Uniform State Laws (NCCUSL) on July 23, 1999. A copy of UETA is available at www.law.upenn.edu/bll/ulc/fnact99/1990s/ueta99.htm.

[41] Directive 1999/93/EC of 13 December 1999 on a Community Framework for Electronic Signatures (hereinafter "Electronic Signatures Directive"). A copy of the Electronic Signatures Directive is available at www.signatur.rtr.at/repository/legal-directive-20000119-en.pdf.

[42] The 2005 United Nations Convention on the Use of Electronic Communications in International Contracts (hereinafter "UN Convention") is an international treaty negotiated at the United Nations Commission on International Trade Law (UNCITRAL) between 2002 and 2005 and adopted by the U.N. General Assembly on November 23, 2005. It is intended to remove obstacles to the use of electronic communications in international contracting, including obstacles that might arise from differing country-specific approaches to e-commerce, and obstacles arising under existing international trade law instruments, most of which were negotiated long before the development of electronic commerce technology. The Convention applies only to business-to-business transactions in international commerce. A copy of the UN text is available at www.uncitral.org/uncitral/en/uncitral_texts/electronic_commerce/2005Convention.html

[43] E-SIGN, 15 USC § 101(d); UETA § 12. In the US these same security requirements are also necessary to satisfy legal record retention obligations. Id.

displayed to the person to whom it is to be made available."[44]

The bottom line, however, is that the admissibility of all types of electronic data may ultimately depend on the level of information security provided in order to ensure that the integrity and availability of the information remains intact.

3.5 Who is responsible for security?

Protecting the security of corporate information and computer systems was once just a technical issue to be addressed by the IT department. Today, however, as information security has evolved into a legal obligation, responsibility for compliance has been put directly on the shoulders of senior management, and in many cases the board of directors. It is, in many respects, a corporate governance issue.[45]

US law in particular, has required senior management to take direct responsibility for security. Under the Sarbanes-Oxley Act, for example, responsibility lies with the CEO and the CFO.[46] In the financial industry, the GLB Security Regulations place responsibility for security directly with the board of directors.[47] In the healthcare industry, the HIPAA Security Regulations require an identified security official to be responsible for compliance.[48] Several FTC consent decrees involving companies in a variety of non-

---

[44] UN Convention, Article 9(4).

[45] See e.g. National Association of Corporate Directors, *Information Security Oversight* (2007).

[46] Sarbanes-Oxley Act, Section 302.

[47] See e.g. GLB Security Regulations (Federal Reserve) 12 CFR 208, Appendix D-2.III(A).

[48] HIPAA Security Regulations, 45 CFR Section 164.308(a)(2).

regulated industries do likewise.[49] And federal law places the responsibility for information security within each government agency on the head of such agency.[50]

Evolving case law also suggests that, by virtue of their fiduciary obligations to the company, corporate directors will find that their duty of care includes responsibility for the security of the company's information systems. In particular, it may "extend from safeguarding corporate financial data accuracy to safeguarding the integrity of all stored data."[51] In the *Caremark International Inc. Derivative Litigation*, for example, the Delaware court noted that "it is important that the board exercise a good faith judgment that the corporation's information and reporting system is in concept and design adequate to assure the board that appropriate information will come to its attention in a timely manner as a matter of ordinary operations, so that it may satisfy its responsibility."[52] And in *Bell v. Michigan Council*, liability was imposed where the Board was aware of the risk, but failed to take action.[53]

The private sector is also beginning to recognize that the responsibility for security lies with upper management and the board of directors. The Business Roundtable, for example, has noted both that "[i]nformation security

---

[49] See *FTC Decisions and Consent Decrees* listed in Appendix, including Microsoft Consent Decree at II, p. 4; Ziff Davis Assurance of Discontinuance, Para. 27(a), p. 7; Eli Lilly Decision at II.A.

[50] FISMA, 44 USC 3544(a).

[51] E. Michael Power and Roland L. Trope, *Sailing in Dangerous Waters: A Director's Guide to Data Governance*, American Bar Association (2005), p. 13; Roland L. Trope, "Directors' Digital Fiduciary Duties," IEEE Security & Privacy, January/February 2005 p. 78.

[52] *Caremark International Inc. Derivative Litigation*, 698 A.2d 959 (Del. Ch. 1996).

[53] *Bell v. Michigan Council*, 2005 Mich. App. Lexis 353 (Mich. App. 15 February 2005), pp. 11-13 (noting that harm was foreseeable, but Board took no action).

3: The General Duty to Provide Security

requires CEO attention" and that "[b]oards of directors should consider information security as an essential element of corporate governance and a top priority for board review."[54] The Corporate Governance Task Force Report has taken a similar position, noting that:

The board of directors/trustees or similar governance entity should provide strategic oversight regarding information security, including:

- Understanding the criticality of information and information security to the organization.
- Reviewing investment in information security for alignment with the organization strategy and risk profile.
- Endorsing the development and implementation of a comprehensive information security program.
- Requiring regular reports from management on the program's adequacy and effectiveness.[55]

The scope of that responsibility can also be significant. The GLB Security Regulations, for example, require the board

---

[54] Business Roundtable, *Securing Cyberspace: Business Roundtable's Framework for the Future*, May 19, 2004 pp. 1, 2; available at www.businessroundtable.org/pdf//20040518000CyberSecurityPrinciples.pdf. The Business Roundtable is an association of chief executive officers of leading US corporations with a combined workforce of more than 10 million employees in the United States. See www.businessroundtable.org.

[55] Corporate Governance Task Force Report, National Cyber Security Partnership, *Information Security Governance: A Call to Action*, April 2004, pp. 12-13, available at www.cyberpartnership.org/InfoSecGov4_04.pdf. The National Cyber Security Partnership (NCSP) is led by the Business Software Alliance (BSA), the Information Technology Association of America (ITAA), TechNet and the US Chamber of Commerce in voluntary partnership with academicians, CEOs, federal government agencies and industry experts. Following the release of the 2003 White House National Strategy to Secure Cyberspace and the National Cyber Security Summit, this public-private partnership was established to develop shared strategies and programs to better secure and enhance America's critical information infrastructure. Further information is available at www.cyberpartnership.org.

of directors to approve the written security program, to oversee the development, implementation, and maintenance of the program, and to require regular reports (e.g. at least annually) regarding the overall status of the security program, the company's compliance with regulations, and material matters relating to the security program.[56]

Similarly, under the Federal Information Security Management Act (FISMA), the head of each government agency is responsible for providing information security protections, complying with the requirements of the statute, and ensuring that information security management processes are integrated within agency strategic and operational planning processes. The head of each agency is also required to appropriately delegate implementation tasks to the CIO and others. The HIPAA Security Regulations require that an identified security official be responsible for developing and implementing the required policies and procedures.

---

[56] GLB Security Regulations (OCC), 12 CFR Part 30, Appendix B, Part III.A and Part III.F.

CHAPTER 4: THE LEGAL STANDARD FOR COMPLIANCE

The general obligation to provide security for data is often simply stated in the law as an obligation to provide "reasonable" or "appropriate" security designed to achieve certain objectives. In some cases, statutes and regulations define those objectives in terms of positive results to be achieved, such as ensuring the *availability* of systems and information, controlling *access* to systems and information, and ensuring the *confidentiality, integrity,* and *authenticity* of information.[1] In other cases, they define those objectives in terms of the harms to be avoided – e.g. to protect systems and information against unauthorized access, use, disclosure or transfer, modification or alteration, processing, and accidental loss or destruction.[2] And in some cases, no objectives are stated.

---

[1] See e.g. in the US FISMA, 44 USC Section 3542(b)(1); GLB Security Regulations (OCC), 12 CFR Part 30 Appendix B, Part II.B; HIPAA Security Regulations, 45 CFR Section 164.306(a)(1); Microsoft Consent Decree at II, p. 4; in other countries, Argentina Act, Section 9(2); Estonia Act, Section 19(1); Italy Act, Annex B, Section 19.4; Liechtenstein Ordinance, Article 9.

[2] See e.g. in the US HIPAA Security Regulations, 45 CFR Sections 164.306(a)(2) and (3); FISMA, 44 USC Section 3542(b)(1); 44 USC Section 3532(b)(1). Most privacy laws in other countries also focus their security requirements from this perspective. This includes, for example, the EU Data Protection Directive, Article 17(1); Albania Act, Article 9; Argentina Act, Article 9(1); Australia Act, Schedule 3, Section 4.1; Austria Act, Section 14(1); Belgium Act, Art. 16(4); Canada Act, Schedule 1, Section 4.7.1; Denmark Act, Section 41(3); Estonia Act, Section 19(1) and (2); Finland Act, Section 32(1); France Act, Article 34; German Act, Annex (to the first sentence of Section 9), Sections 1, 2, and 4; Greece Act, Article 10(3); Hong Kong Act, Principle 4; Hungary Act, Article 10(2); Ireland Act, Section 2-(1)(d), and First Schedule, Article 7; Italy Act, Section 31; Lithuania Act, Article 24(1); Netherlands Act, Article 13; Philippines Act, Article 8.1; Poland Act, Articles 7 and 36; Portugal Act, Article 14(1); Russia Act, Section 19(1); Singapore Model Code, Principle 7, Section 4.7.1; Slovakia Act, Section

Regardless of approach, achieving these objectives involves implementing security controls designed to protect systems and information from the various threats they face. What those threats are, where they come from, what is at risk, and how serious the consequences are, will of course, vary greatly from case to case. But responding to the threats a company faces with appropriate physical, technical, and organizational security measures is the focus of the duty to provide security.

The key issue for companies that must comply is determining the scope of this obligation. Just what exactly is the business required to do? Does it need to install a firewall? How many characters should be required for passwords? Is it necessary to encrypt company data? Is it OK for employees to take laptops home?

Unfortunately, laws and regulations rarely specify what specific security measures a business should implement to satisfy its legal obligations.[3] Typically, they simply require the company to establish and maintain internal security "procedures," "controls," "safeguards," or "measures" directed toward achieving the goals or objectives identified above, but often without any further direction or guidance.

As a result, the nature of the legal obligation to address security is often poorly understood by those levels in management charged with the responsibility, by the technical experts who must implement it, and by the lawyers who must ensure compliance. Yet, understanding

---

15(1); Spain Act, Article 9; United Arab Emirates Act, Articles 15(1) and 16(1); UK Act, Schedule 1, Part I, Seventh Principle.

[3] Although, as discussed in Chapter 6, they often do specify the *categories* of security controls that the business must consider. See e.g. HIPAA Security Regulations, 45 CFR Part 164.

the legal standard for compliance is perhaps one of the most critical security issues a company will face.

4.1 Recognition that security is relative

Defining the scope of a company's security obligations begins with understanding that the law views security as a relative concept. That view is evident from the fact that most laws and regulations simply require that the security be "reasonable," "appropriate," "suitable," "necessary," or "adequate."

In Europe, for example, the Data Protection Directive requires the controllers of personal data to:

...implement *appropriate* technical and organizational measures to protect personal data against accidental or unlawful destruction or accidental loss, alteration, unauthorized disclosure or access, in particular where the processing involves the transmission of data over a network, and against all other unlawful forms of processing.[4]

Thus, country implementations of the EU Data Protection Directive generally require the use of security measures that are *appropriate* to protect the personal data[5] or that are *necessary* to protect the personal data.[6]

---

[4] EU Data Protection Directive, Article 17(1) (emphasis added).

[5] See e.g. Belgium Act, Article 16(4); Denmark Act, Section 41(3); Estonia Act, Section 19(2); Greece Act, Article 10(3); Iceland Rules, Article 4; Ireland Act, Section 2.-(1)(d) and First Schedule Article 7; Liechtenstein Act, Article 9; Lithuania Act, Article 24(1); Netherlands Act, Article 13; Poland Act, Article 7; Portugal Act, Article 14(1); Slovakia Act, Section 15(1); Sweden Act, Section 31; and UK Act, Schedule 1, Part 1, Seventh Principle.

[6] See e.g. Finland Act, Section 32(1); Germany Act, Section 9; Hungary Act, Article 10(1); Italy Act, Sections 31 and 33; Spain Act, Article 9.

Most other countries also use the *appropriate* standard in their security laws,[7] although some use other variations, such as requiring security measures *reasonable under the circumstances*,[8] requiring *useful precautions*,[9] requiring *all practical steps*,[10] and requiring *necessary and proper measures*.[11]

In the US, the Privacy Protection Act of 1974[12] requires government agencies that maintain a system of records about an individual to:

... establish *appropriate* administrative, technical, and physical safeguards to insure the security and confidentiality of records and to protect against any anticipated threats or hazards to their security or integrity which could result in substantial harm, embarrassment, inconvenience, or unfairness to any individual on whom information is maintained.[13]

Other laws applicable to the private sector take a similar approach. HIPAA requires *"reasonable and appropriate"* security.[14] The GLB Security Regulations require financial institutions to "implement a comprehensive written information security program that includes administrative, technical, and physical safeguards *appropriate* to the size and complexity of the bank and the nature and scope of its

---

[7] See e.g. Albania Act, Article 9; Bahamas Act, Article 6.1(d); Canada Act, Schedule 1, Section 4.7 Principle 7; Isle of Man Act, Schedule 1, Articles 17 and 21; Malta Act, Article 26; Mauritius Act, Article 27(1); Philippines Act, Article 8.1; Singapore Model Guidelines, Article 4.7 Principle 7; United Arab Emirates Act, Article 15(1).

[8] Australia Act, Schedule 3, Section 4.1; Russia Act, Section 19(1).

[9] France Act, Article 34.

[10] Hong Kong Act, Principle 4.

[11] Japan Act, Article 20.

[12] 5 USC Sec. 552a. This statute applies only to government agencies.

[13] 5 USC § 552a (d)(10) (emphasis added).

[14] 42 USC 1320d-2(d)(2).

activities."[15] And many of the state personal information security laws in the US generally require "*reasonable* security procedures and practices."[16]

The most recent international legal effort, the 2005 UN Convention on the Use of Electronic Communications in International Contracts, also expressly adopts the view that security is a relative concept. In addressing requirements for electronic signatures, the Convention requires that the method used to authenticate the identity of a party signing a contract and to indicate the party's intent must either be "as reliable as appropriate for the purpose" or "proven in fact." In addressing the requirements for originality of electronic records, the Convention requires only that there exist "a reliable assurance as to the integrity of the information." And it makes clear that "the standard of reliability required shall be assessed in the light of the purpose for which the information was generated and in the light of all the relevant circumstances." Like most other laws, the UN Convention does not in any way require the use of any specific security measures or technologies.[17]

By adopting this approach, the laws recognize that the choice of security measures and technology can (and should) vary depending on the situation. Thus, most laws do not require companies to implement any specific security controls (such as a firewall), nor do they specify any safe harbors (e.g. if you implement a firewall you will

---

[15] See Gramm-Leach-Bliley Act (GLB), Public Law 106-102, §§ 501 and 505(b), 15 USC §§ 6801, 6805, and GLB Security Regulations at 12 CFR Part 30, Appendix B (OCC), 12 CFR Part 208, Appendix D (Federal Reserve System), 12 CFR Part 364, Appendix B (FDIC), 12 CFR Part 568 (Office of Thrift Supervision) and 16 CFR Part 314 (FTC) (emphasis added).

[16] See e.g. Cal. Civil Code § 1798.81.5(b).

[17] See UN Electronic Communications Convention at Article 9(3), 9(4), and 9(5).

be compliant). But security laws often do require companies to address certain *categories* of security controls[18] (such as access control), while leaving to the company the decision as to whether using a specific control (e.g. a firewall) will provide adequate security to address that control category.

4.2 Legal definition of "reasonable security"

Although the law views security as a relative concept, and provides businesses with little or no specific guidance as to what is required for legal compliance, developments over the past few years suggest that a definition of the legal standard for "reasonable" security is clearly emerging. That standard rejects requirements for specific one-size-fits-all security measures (such as firewalls, passwords, encryption, or the like), and instead adopts a fact-specific approach to corporate security obligations that requires a "process" applied to the unique facts of each case. As noted in one opinion:

The reasonableness standard . . . is . . . not technically or operationally prescriptive. It does not specify particular technologies or procedures that must be used to protect personal information. The reasonableness standard recognizes that, because situations vary, the measures needed to protect personal information vary. It also accommodates technological changes and the challenges and solutions that they bring to bear on, and offer for, personal information security.[19]

---

[18] See Chapter 6.
[19] *Eastern School District*, Report P-2008-002, Office of the Information and Privacy Commissioner, Newfoundland and Labrador, 23 July 2008, p. 14, available at www.oipc.gov.nl.ca/pdf/P-2008-002_Eastern%20School%20District.pdf.

Thus, rather than requiring companies to implement specific security measures, the legal standard requires companies to engage in an *ongoing and repetitive process.* That process involves assessing the specific risks a company faces, identifying and implementing appropriate security controls responsive to those risks, verifying that they are effectively implemented, and ensuring that they are continually updated in response to new developments. The results of that process, rather than the text of any specific law or regulation, will determine the specific security controls a company must implement to be legally compliant.

As a consequence, the presence or absence of specific security measures says little about the status of a company's legal compliance with its information security obligations. Because armed guards at the front of a building do not protect against hackers accessing information through the Internet, and because firewalls designed to stop hackers do not protect against dishonest employees with authorized access, the law puts its focus on implementing those security measures that respond to the specific threats a business faces. It recognizes that there are a variety of different appropriate security measures responsive to specific threats, and recognizes that threats (and appropriate responsive security measures) vary from business to business, and are constantly changing.

Based on a review of available security laws, regulations, court decisions, and consent decrees, the essence of the legally-required process-oriented approach to security compliance becomes clear. In fact, while some laws contain much more detail than others, what emerges is an amazing consistency among most security statutes and regulations.

At its essence, the legal standard for information security requires companies to implement a comprehensive (and written) information security program whereby the company:

- identifies its information and system assets;
- conducts periodic risk assessments to identify the specific threats to those assets the company faces, its vulnerabilities to those threats, and the harm that would result if the threats materialize;
- selects and implements appropriate security controls to manage and control the risks identified;
- monitors and tests the program to ensure that it is effective;
- continually reviews and adjusts the program in light of ongoing changes, including obtaining regular independent audits and reporting where appropriate; and
- oversees third party service provider arrangements.

A key aspect of this process is recognition that it is never completed. It is ongoing, and must be continually reviewed, revised, and updated. As noted in guidance issued by the US federal banking regulators:

Organizations often inaccurately perceive information security as the state or condition of controls at a point in time. Security is an ongoing process, whereby the condition of a financial institution's controls is just one indicator of its overall security posture. Other indicators include the ability of the institution to continually assess its posture and react appropriately in the face of rapidly changing threats, technologies, and business conditions. A financial institution establishes and maintains truly effective information security when it continuously integrates processes, people, and technology to mitigate risk in accordance with risk assessment and acceptable risk tolerance levels. Financial institutions protect their information by instituting a security process that *identifies* risks, forms a strategy to *manage* the risks, *implements* the strategy, *tests* the implementation, and *monitors* the environment to control the risks.[20]

4.3 Adoption of the legal definition

In the US, this "process-oriented" legal standard for corporate information security was first set forth in a series of financial industry security regulations required under the US Gramm-Leach-Bliley Act (GLBA) titled *Guidelines Establishing Standards for Safeguarding Consumer Information*. They were issued by the four primary US banking regulatory agencies (the Federal Reserve, the OCC, FDIC, and the Office of Thrift Supervision) on February 1, 2001,[21] and later adopted by the FTC in its GLB *Safeguards Rule* on May 23, 2002.[22] The same approach was also incorporated in the Federal Information Security Management Act of 2002 (FISMA),[23] and in the HIPAA *Security Standards* issued by the Department of Health and Human Services on February 20, 2003.[24]

The FTC has since adopted the view that the process-oriented approach to information security outlined in these regulations sets forth a general "best practice" for legal compliance that should apply to all businesses in all industries.[25] Thus, it has, implemented this process-

---

[20] FFIEC, *IT Examinations Handbook: Information Security* (July 2006) p. 1 (emphasis in original).

[21] 66 Fed. Reg. 8616, February 1, 2001; 12 CFR Part 30, Appendix B (OCC), 12 CFR Part 208, Appendix D (Federal Reserve System), 12 CFR Part 364, Appendix B (FDIC), 12 CFR Part 568 (Office of Thrift Supervision).

[22] 67 Fed. Reg. 36484, 23 May 2002; 16 CFR Part 314.

[23] 44 USC Section 3544(b).

[24] 45 CFR Parts 164.

[25] See Prepared Statement of the Federal Trade Commission on Identity Theft: Innovative Solutions For An Evolving Problem, Presented by Lydia Parnes, Director, Bureau of

oriented approach in all of its decisions and consent decrees relating to alleged failures to provide appropriate information security.[26]

The National Association of Insurance Commissioners has also recommended the same approach, and to date, several state insurance regulators have adopted it.[27] Several state Attorneys General have also adopted this approach in their actions against perceived offenders.[28] And now we are starting to see some cases take the same approach.[29]

In *Guin v. Brazos Education*, for example, the court rejected the view that the law requires specific security measures (in that case, encryption). Instead, it focused on the fact that the defendant had followed the proper "process" – i.e. had put in place written security policies, had done current risk assessments, and had implemented proper safeguards as required by the GLB Act. And because the defendant had properly followed such a

---

Consumer Protection, Before the Subcommittee On Terrorism, Technology and Homeland Security of the Senate Committee on the Judiciary, United States Senate, 21 March 2007 p. 7 (noting that "the FTC Safeguards Rule promulgated under the GLB Act serves as a good model" for satisfying the obligation to maintain reasonable and appropriate security); available at www.ftc.gov/os/testimony/P065409identitytheftsenate03212007.pdf. See also, Prepared Statement of the Federal Trade Commission before the Subcommittee on Technology, Information Policy, Intergovernmental Relations, and the Census, Committee on Government Reform, US House of Representatives on "Protecting Our Nation's Cyberspace," 21 April 2004, p. 5 (noting that "security is an ongoing process of using reasonable and appropriate measures in light of the circumstances"), available at www.ftc.gov/os/2004/04/042104cybersecuritytestimony.pdf.

[26] See e.g. FTC Decisions and Consent Decrees listed in the Appendix.

[27] See e.g. National Association of Insurance Commissioners, *Standards for Safeguarding Customer Information Model Regulation*, IV-673-1 available at www.naic.org (adopted in at least 9 states so far).

[28] See e.g. state Attorneys General consent decrees listed in the Appendix.

[29] See e.g. *Guin v. Brazos Higher Education Service*, Civ. No. 05-668, 2006 US Dist. Lexis 4846 (D. Minn. Feb. 7, 2006) and *Bell v. Michigan Council*, 2005 Mich. App. LEXIS 353 (Mich. App. 15 February 2005).

process, the court held there was no liability for a breach that did occur.[30] Conversely, in *Bell v. Michigan Council*, the court imposed liability where the defendant was aware of the security risk, but did nothing to address it.[31]

The New Jersey Advisory Committee on Professional Ethics also briefly addressed this issue of reasonable security in the context of an opinion on attorney use of technology to store client information for remote access. Noting the ethical obligation of the attorney to "exercise reasonable care" against the possibility of unauthorized access to client information, the Committee noted that "reasonable care," "does not mean that the lawyer absolutely and strictly guarantees that the information will be utterly invulnerable against all unauthorized access." Moreover, the Committee rejected requirements for specific technical solutions. Instead, it noted that the touchstone of reasonable care is that "use is made of available technology to guard against reasonably foreseeable attempts to infiltrate the data."[32]

In the EU, the process-oriented approach noted above is specifically referenced in some statutes,[33] and impliedly incorporated in others through requirements for a risk-based analysis *(see Section 5.2)*. In addition, several statutes incorporate the various elements of the process, including

---

[30] *Guin v. Brazos Higher Education Service*, Civ. No. 05-668, 2006 US Dist. Lexis 4846 (D. Minn. 7 February 2006).

[31] *Bell v. Michigan Council*, 2005 Mich. App. Lexis 353 (Mich. App. 15 February 2005).

[32] New Jersey Advisory Committee on Professional Ethics, Opinion 701 (2006) available at
www.judiciary.state.nj.us/notices/ethics/ACPE_Opinion701_ElectronicStorage_1202200
5.pdf.

[33] From Appendix See e.g. Italy Act, Annex B, § 19.3; Slovakia Act, § 16(5).

conducting periodic risk assessments,[34] developing and implementing a responsive security program[35] including employee training and education,[36] monitoring and testing the program,[37] continually reviewing and adjusting the program,[38] and overseeing third party service provider arrangements.[39]

Overall, the trend is to recognize what security consultants have been saying for some time: "security is a process, not a product."[40] Even the international security standard ISO27001 takes a similar approach, stating that it: "adopts a *process approach* for establishing, implementing, operating, monitoring, reviewing, maintaining and improving an organization's [information security management system]."[41]

---

[34] From Appendix, see Italy Act, Annex B, Section 19.3; Slovak Republic Act, Section 16(5).

[35] From Appendix, see Argentina Act, Article 9(1); Estonia Act, Section 19(1); Belgium Act, Art. 16(4); Denmark Act, Section 41(3); Estonia Act, Section 19(1) (IT); Finland Act, Section 32(1); German Act, Section 9; Greece Act, Article 10(3); Hungary Act, Article 10(1); Lithuania Act, Article 24(1); Netherlands Act, Article 13; Portugal Act, Article 14(1); Slovak Republic Act, Section 15(1); Spain Act, Article 9; Sweden Act, Section 31; UK Act, Schedule 1, Part I, Seventh Principle; Swiss Act, Article 7.

[36] From Appendix, see Australia Act, Schedule 2, Section 3.1(b); Belgium Act, Art 16(2)(3); Canada Act, Schedule 1, 4.7 Principle 7, Clause 4.7.4; Estonia Act, Section 20(3); Ireland Act, Section 2C(2); Italy Act, Annex B, Sections 4 and 19.6; Slovak Republic Act, Sections 17 and 19(3).

[37] From Appendix, see German Act, Section 9a (audit); Poland Ordinance, Attachment A (Basic Security Measures) § VII (monitor); Slovak Republic Act, Section 16(6)(d); Spain Royal Decree 1720/2007, Article 96 (Medium-level security measures) (audit).

[38] From Appendix, see Spain Royal Decree 1720/2007, Article 88.

[39] From Appendix, see Australia Act, Section 14, Principle 4; Austria Act, Article 15(2); Belgium Act, Article 16; Denmark Act, Sections 41 and 42; Estonia Act, Section 20; Finland Act, Section 32(2); Ireland Act, Section 2C-(3); Italy Act, Annex B, Sections 4 and 19.6; Slovak Republic Act, Sections 17 and 19(3).

[40] Bruce Schneier, *Secrets & Lies: Digital Security in a Networked World* (John Wiley & Sons, 2000), page XII.

[41] ISO27001, Section 0.2, page v.

In sum, legal compliance with security obligations involves a "process" applied to the facts of each case in order to achieve an objective (i.e. to identify and implement the security measures appropriate for that situation), rather than the implementation of standard specific security measures in all cases. There are generally no hard and fast rules requiring specific security controls. Instead, the legal obligation regarding security focuses on what is reasonable under the circumstances to achieve the desired security objectives. Consequently, the legal standard focuses on requiring businesses to develop comprehensive information security programs, but leaves the details to the facts and circumstances of each case.

Chapters 5 and 6 address implementation of this legal standard to develop a compliant security program.

CHAPTER 5: DEVELOPING A COMPLIANT SECURITY PROGRAM

Implementing legally-compliant "reasonable security" requires the development of an appropriate comprehensive information security program. While much has been written about developing an information security program from a technical perspective, this chapter will focus on the legal requirements.

As noted in Chapter 4, developing a legally-compliant information security program involves an iterative process that requires that a company do the following:

- Identify its information and system assets.
- Conduct periodic risk assessments to:
    - ✓ identify the specific threats to those assets the company faces,
    - ✓ identify its vulnerabilities to those threats, and
    - ✓ estimate the resulting harm if a threat materializes and exploits a vulnerability.
- Identify and implement security controls:
    - ✓ by considering the *categories of security controls* identified in applicable laws,
    - ✓ in light of the results of the risk assessment and other relevant factors.
- Monitor and test the program to ensure that it is effective.
- Continually review and adjust the program in light of ongoing changes.
- Oversee third party service provider arrangements.

The following sections discuss each of those requirements in detail.

As a threshold matter, however, it should be noted that the security program must be in writing. Numerous regulators take the view that "if the security program is not in writing, it doesn't exist." But more importantly, many laws and regulations expressly require that the security program be in writing.[1]

5.1 Identify information assets

In order to protect something, you need to know what it is, where it is, how it is used, how valuable it is, and so forth. Thus, when addressing information security, the first step is to identify the information assets to be protected and define the scope of the effort.

This involves taking an inventory of the data and information that that company creates, collects, receives, uses, processes, stores, and communicates to others. It also requires examining the systems, networks and processes by which such data is created, collected, received, used, processed, stored, and communicated.

The process requires more than merely identifying data and systems, however. It is also important to understand where the data and systems are located. This means identifying

---

[1] In the US see e.g. GLB Security Regulations, 12 CFR Part 30 Appendix B, Part II.A; HIPAA Security Regulations, 45 CFR Section 164.316(b)(1); FISMA, 44 USC Section 3544(b). In other countries, See e.g. Argentina Regulations of the National Bureau for the Protection of Personal Data; Austria Act, Article 14(2)(8); EU Directive, Article 17(4); Iceland Rules, Article 3; Italy Act, Section 34(1); Liechtenstein Ordinance, Article 12; Lithuania Act, Article 24; Netherlands Act, Article 14(5); Norway Act, Section 13; Philippines Act, Section 8.1; Poland Act, Article 36; Portugal Act, Article 14(4); Slovenia Act, Article 25(2); Spain Royal Decree 1720/2007, Article 88.

where in the company (e.g. which office and which department), the data and systems are located, and who controls them. It also requires identifying in which jurisdictions (country and state or province) they are collected, processed, and stored, as this will impact which laws must be complied with.

As is often the case, little known but sensitive data files are often found in a variety of places within the company. Moreover, it is also important to consider company data that is in the possession and control of a third party, such as an outsource service provider. As discussed in Section 5.6 below, the company is still responsible for the security of its data in the possession of third parties.

5.2 Conduct a risk assessment

Implementing a comprehensive security program to protect a company's information assets requires a thorough assessment of the potential risks to the organization's information systems and data. Thus, once the company has identified the systems and data to be protected, it must undertake a risk assessment process to identify and assess the risks to those systems and data.

Assessing risks requires consideration of threats and vulnerabilities.

A *threat* is anything that has the potential to cause harm. It can be an act of nature, such as a fire, flood, or tornado, or it can be man-made, such as a computer virus, the actions of a hacker, or the negligent mistake of an employee.

A *vulnerability* is a flaw or weakness that can be accidentally triggered or intentionally exploited by the threat to endanger or cause harm to an information asset. It might be a hole in the roof, a system with easy to guess passwords, unencrypted data on a laptop computer, disgruntled employees, or employees that simply do not understand what steps they need to take to protect the security of company data.

The likelihood that a threat will exploit a vulnerability to cause harm creates a risk. Stated differently, where a threat intersects with a vulnerability, risk is present. For example, if the threat is rain, and the vulnerability is a hole in the roof, risk is the likelihood that it will rain, causing water to enter the building through the hole in the roof, and doing damage to the building and/or its contents. Similarly, if the threat is a hacker, and the vulnerability is open Internet access to a server containing sensitive data, risk is the likelihood that a hacker will enter the system and view, copy, alter, or destroy the sensitive data.

In other words, *risk* is the likelihood that something bad will happen that causes harm to an information asset. Somewhat more precisely, "Risk is a function of the likelihood of a given threat-source's exercising a particular potential vulnerability, and the resulting impact of that adverse event on the organization."[2]

Risk assessment, then, is the process of identifying vulnerabilities and threats to the information assets used by the company, and assessing the potential impact/harm that would result if a threat materializes. This forms the basis on which the company determines what countermeasures (i.e. security controls), if any, it should implement to reduce

---

[2] NIST Special Publication 800-30, *Risk Management Guide for Information Technology Systems* (July 2002) p. 8.

risk to an acceptable level. Thus, a risk assessment requires:

- conducting a threat assessment to identify all reasonably foreseeable internal and external threats to the information and system assets to be protected;[3]
- conducting a vulnerability assessment to identify the company's vulnerabilities;
- assessing the likelihood that each of the threats will materialize, and if so, the probability that it will exploit one or more of the vulnerabilities to cause harm – i.e. identifying the likelihood that threat sources with the potential to exploit weaknesses or vulnerabilities in the system will actually do so;
- evaluating the potential damage that will result in such a case; and
- assessing the sufficiency of the security controls in place to guard against the threat.[4]

This process will be the baseline against which security controls can be selected, implemented, measured, and validated. The goal is to understand the risks the business faces, and determine what level of risk is acceptable, in order to identify appropriate and cost-effective safeguards to combat that risk.

Traditional negligence law essentially takes the same approach. That is, in assessing what qualifies as reasonable care in a given case, negligence law identifies the relevant factors as: (1) the probability of the identified harm

---

[3] See e.g. GLB Security Regulations, 12 CFR Part 30, Appendix B, Part III.B(1).
[4] See e.g. FISMA, 44 USC Sections 3544(a)(2)(A) and 3544(b)(1); GLB Security Regulations, 12 CFR Part 30, Appendix B, Part III.B(2).

occurring (i.e. the likelihood that a foreseeable threat will materialize); (2) the gravity of the resulting injury if the threat does materialize; and (3) the burden of implementing adequate precautions.[5] In other words, the standard of care to be exercised in any particular case depends upon the circumstances of that case and on the extent of foreseeable danger.[6]

Numerous security laws and regulations expressly require a risk assessment as part of a comprehensive security program. And laws and regulations that do not expressly include such a requirement typically do so impliedly.

In the US, a risk assessment is expressly required by a variety of statutes and regulations, such as GLB, HIPAA, and FISMA. And it is impliedly required by most other security statutes and regulations by imposing an obligation to provide "reasonable" security. Likewise, the consent decrees entered in all FTC enforcement actions have expressly extended the banking and healthcare sector-specific requirements for a risk assessment to all industries generally.[7]

In addition, several US courts have held that a risk assessment plays a key role in determining whether a duty will be imposed and liability found. In the case of *Wolfe v. MBNA America Bank*, for example, a bank issued a credit card to an imposter who had stolen the plaintiff's identity. The court held that the injury to the plaintiff resulting from the bank's negligent issuance of a credit card was both

---

[5] See e.g. *United States v. Carroll Towing*, 159 F.2d 169, 173 (2d Cir. 1947).
[6] See e.g. *DCR Inc. v. Peak Alarm Co.* 663 P.2d 433, 435 (Utah 1983); *see also Glatt v. Feist*, 156 N.W.2d 819, 829 (N.D. 1968) (the amount or degree of diligence necessary to constitute ordinary care varies with facts and circumstances of each case).
[7] See list in Appendix.

foreseeable and preventable, and that as a consequence "the defendant has a duty to verify the authenticity and accuracy of a credit account application."[8] In other words, where a risk assessment would have identified a risk of harm, a company has a duty to defend against it.

Similarly, in *Bell v. Michigan Council*, the court held that where a harm was foreseeable, and the potential severity of the risk was high, the defendant was liable for failure to provide appropriate security to address the potential harm.[9] On the other hand, in *Guin v. Brazos Education*, the court held that where a proper risk assessment was done, but a particular harm was not reasonably foreseeable, the defendant would not be liable for failure to defend against it.[10]

In the EU and other countries, a risk assessment is almost always a required element of the obligation to provide appropriate data security. Many data protection laws expressly require a risk assessment, including the data protection laws in Iceland, Italy, Norway, and the Slovak Republic.[11] Most such laws, however, impliedly require a risk assessment. They typically do this by requiring that the company must provide a level of security "appropriate to the risk." Countries that take this approach include Albania, Austria, France, Hong Kong, Ireland, Isle of Man, Italy, Jersey, Lithuania, Mauritius, Philippines, Poland,

---

[8] *Wolfe v. MBNA America Bank*, 485 F.Supp.2d 874, 882 (W.D. Tenn. 2007).
[9] See *Bell v. Michigan Council*, 2005 Mich. App. Lexis 353 (Mich. App. 15 February 2005).
[10] See *Guin v. Brazos Higher Education Service*, Civ. No. 05-668, 2006 US Dist. Lexis 4846 at *13 (D. Minn. Feb. 7, 2006) (finding that where a proper risk assessment was done, the inability to foresee and deter a specific burglary of a laptop was not a breach of a duty of reasonable care).
[11] From Appendix, see Iceland law, Article 11; Italy law, Annex B, Section 19.3; Norway regulations, Section 2-4; and Slovak Republic law, Section 16.5.

Portugal, Romania, Singapore, Spain, United Arab Emirates, and the United Kingdom.[12]

In most cases, however, the law does not generally specify how to do a risk assessment. In the US the banking regulators have referred financial institutions seeking general information on risk assessments to:[13] (1) the *Small Entity Compliance Guide for the Interagency Guidelines Establishing Information Security Standards,*[14] and (2) the *FFIEC IT Examination Handbook, Information Security Booklet.*[15] The US National Institute of Standards and Technology (NIST) also offers guidance on conducting risk assessments,[16] and there is now an ISO/IEC risk assessment standard as well.[17]

---

[12] From Appendix, See e.g. Albania law Article 9; Austria law Section 14(2).8; EU Data Protection Directive Article 17(1); France law Article 34; Hong Kong law Principle 4; Ireland law Section 2C.-(1); Isle of Man law Schedule 1; Italy law Section 32(1); Jersey law Seventh Principle; Lithuania law Article 24; Mauritius law Section 27(1); Philippines law Article 8.1; Poland law Article 36; Portugal law Article 14(1); Romania law Article 20(2); Singapore Model Code Principle 7, 4.7.2; Spain law Article 9; United Arab Emirates law Articles 15(2) and 16(2); and the United Kingdom law Seventh Principle.

[13] FFIEC, *Frequently Asked Questions on FFIEC Guidance on Authentication in an Internet Banking Environment,* August 8, 2006 p. 5, available at www.ffiec.gov/pdf/authentication_faq.pdf.

[14] *Small Entity Compliance Guide for the Interagency Guidelines Establishing Information Security Standards,* December 14, 2005, available at www.federalreserve.gov/boarddocs/press/bcreg/2005/20051214/default.htm.

[15] FFIEC, *IT Examination Handbook, Information Security Booklet,* July 2006, available at www.ffiec.gov/ffiecinfobase/booklets/information_security/information_security.pdf.

[16] See NIST Special Publication No. 800-30, *"Risk Management Guide for Information Technology Systems,"* available at http://csrc.nist.gov/publications/nistpubs/800-30/sp800-30.pdf.

[17] See ISO/IEC 27005:2008 *"Information technology – Security techniques – Information security risk management,"* available at http://www.itgovernance.co.uk/standards.aspx.

5.3 Select and implement security controls

The next step in the process of developing a comprehensive information security program is to select and implement appropriate physical, technical, and administrative security controls to manage and control the risks the company faces.[18] This involves considering the *categories of security controls* identified in the applicable security laws (and any additional categories that are suggested by the risk assessment), in light of the results of the risk assessment and other relevant factors, to select specific security controls that will reduce the company's risks and vulnerabilities to a reasonable and appropriate level.[19]

5.3.1 Categories of security controls to consider

Most security statutes and regulations do not require companies to implement any specific security measures or use any particular technology. As expressly stated in the HIPAA Security Regulations, for example, companies "may use any security measures" reasonably designed to achieve the objectives specified in the regulations.[20]

Nonetheless, security statutes and regulations seem to consistently require that companies consider certain

---

[18] See e.g. US GLB Security Regulations (OCC), 12 CFR Part 30 Appendix B, Part II.A; HIPAA Security Regulations, 45 CFR Section 164.308(a)(1)(ii)(B); FISMA, 44 USC Section 3544(b); Belgium Act, Art. 16(4); Denmark Act, Section 41(3); Estonia Act, Section 19(1); EU Data Protection Directive, Article 17(1); Finland Act, Section 32(1); German Act, Section 9; Greece Act, Article 10(3); Hungary Act, Article 10(1); Lithuania Act, Article 24(1); Netherlands Act, Article 13; Philippines Act, Article 8.1; Portugal Act, Article 14(1); Russia Act, Section 19(1); Slovakia Act, Section 15(1); Spain Act, Article 9; Sweden Act, Section 31; United Arab Emirates Act, Articles 15(1) and 16(1); UK Act, Schedule 1, Part 1, Seventh Principle.

[19] See e.g. HIPAA Security Regulations, 45 CFR Section 164.308(a)(1)(ii)(B).

[20] HIPAA Security Regulations, 45 CFR Section 164.306(b)(1).

categories of security measures, even if the way in which each category is addressed is not specified. For example, many laws require companies to implement access control measures to ensure that only authorized persons can access sensitive data. But the laws typically say nothing about which access controls should be used. At most, they will sometimes define objectives or criteria that must be achieved (such as restricting access on a need to know basis, or requiring that access be terminated when an employee leaves the company). Thus (in the example of access controls), companies are free to select any types of access controls that achieve those objectives and are reasonable for the business in light of the results of its risk assessment.

The specific categories of security measures that security statutes and regulations often require companies to consider are listed and discussed in detail in Chapter 6.

5.3.2 *Key role of the risk assessment*

In determining what specific security measures should be implemented within each of those relevant categories of security controls, virtually all of the existing precedents recognize that there is no "one size fits all" approach. Which security measures are appropriate for a particular organization will vary, depending upon a variety of factors.

The primary factor, and the key to providing legally-compliant security, is the requirement that the specific security controls selected and implemented must be responsive to the company's fact-specific risk assessment. In other words, merely implementing seemingly strong security measures is not, by itself, sufficient for legal compliance. Those security controls must be responsive to the particular threats a business faces, and must address its vulnerabilities.

Posting armed guards around a building, for example, sounds impressive as a security measure, but if the primary threat the company faces is unauthorized remote access to its data via the Internet, that particular security measure is of little value. Likewise, firewalls and intrusion detection software are often effective ways to stop hackers and protect sensitive databases, but if a company's major vulnerability is careless (or malicious) employees who inadvertently (or intentionally) disclose passwords or protected information, then even those sophisticated technical security measures, while important, will not adequately address the problem.

In addition to the risk assessment, the following factors are most often cited in security statutes and regulations as relevant to determining what security controls should be implemented in a given case:

- The company's size, complexity, and capabilities.
- The nature and scope of the business activities.
- The nature and sensitivity of the information to be protected.
- The company's technical infrastructure, hardware, and software security capabilities.
- The state of the art regarding technology and security.
- The costs of the security measures.[21]

---

[21] See e.g. From Appendix, US HIPAA Security Regulations, 45 CFR Section 164.306(b)(2); GLB Security Regulations, 12 CFR Part 30 Appendix B, Part II.A and Part II.C; FISMA, 44 USC Sections 3544(a)(2) and 3544(b)(2)(B); Finland Act, Section 32(1);

Interestingly, other than a risk assessment, cost is the one factor mentioned most often, and certainly implies recognition that companies are not required to do everything theoretically possible.

A summary of the process for selecting security controls is found in a guidance document issued by the US banking regulators, which focuses on the selection of security controls regarding authentication of identity by noting the following four key points:[22]

- When offering Internet-based products and services to customers, companies should use effective methods to authenticate the identity of customers using those products and services.
- The authentication techniques employed should be appropriate to the risks associated with those products and services.
- Companies should conduct a risk assessment to identify the types and levels of risk associated with their Internet applications.
- Where risk assessments indicate that the use of single-factor authentication is inadequate, companies should implement multifactor authentication, layered security, or other controls reasonably calculated to mitigate those risks.

The importance of a risk assessment, and its role in determining what specific security controls are appropriate, cannot be overstated. Information security law clearly

---

Ireland Act, Section 2C.-(1); Netherlands Act, Article 13; Portugal Act, Article 14(1); Sweden Act, Section 31; United Arab Emirates Act, Sections 15(2) and 16(2).
[22] FFIEC Guidance, p. 6.

requires companies to use the results of the risk assessment process to identify the appropriate strategy for addressing security controls.

This point was also stressed by the US banking regulators in their response to questions relating to its regulations for strong authentication. When asked whether a financial institution could forgo a risk assessment and move immediately to implement additional strong authentication controls, the regulators responded with an emphatic "no." As they pointed out, the security requirements for authentication are risk-based, and thus, a risk assessment that sufficiently evaluates the risks and identifies the reasons for choosing a particular control should be completed before implementing any particular controls.[23]

The bottom line is that the legal appropriateness of any particular security control is not determined in the abstract. Instead, it must be determined on the basis of a risk assessment specific to the company and its business. Each security control should be appropriate and reasonable, from a business perspective, in light of the reasonably foreseeable risks.

This means, of course, that the standards for legally appropriate security controls will vary across businesses and applications. It also means that what constitutes legally appropriate security controls may also change over time as new threats arise and better technology is developed to address them. Thus, a single risk assessment is never sufficient. Companies must implement an ongoing process

---

[23] See FFIEC, *"Frequently Asked Questions on FFIEC Guidance on Authentication in an Internet Banking Environment,"* August 8, 2006 p. 5, available at www.ncua.gov/letters/2006/CU/06-CU-13_encl.pdf.

to regularly review threats and technology in order to ensure that appropriate changes are implemented as needed.

5.4 Monitor and test the controls

Merely implementing appropriate security measures is not sufficient. Companies must also ensure that the security measures have been properly put in place and are effective. One only need look to the recent security breach involving the TJX Companies – a breach which reportedly involved the compromise of up to 90 million credit card numbers – to see the need for testing. All of the compromised credit card data in that case was apparently encrypted; a fact which might lead many to assume that it was adequately protected. But the weak nature of the encryption used in that case was apparently easily broken by the hackers.

Thus, conducting an assessment of the sufficiency of the security measures in place to control the identified risks,[24] and conducting regular testing or monitoring of the effectiveness of those measures,[25] is an important component of the legal standard. Existing precedent also suggests that companies must monitor compliance with their security programs.[26] To that end, a regular review of records of system activity, such as audit logs, access reports, and security incident tracking reports[27] is also important.

---

[24] From Appendix, Microsoft Consent Decree at II, p. 4.
[25] FISMA, 44 USC Section 3544(b)(5); Eli Lilly Decision at II.C; GLB Security Regulations, 12 CFR Part 30, Appendix B, Part III(c)(3).
[26] From Appendix, Ziff Davis Assurance of Discontinuance, Para. 27(e) and (f), p. 7; Eli Lilly Decision at II.C.
[27] HIPAA Security Regulations, 45 CFR Section 164.308(a)(1)(ii)(D).

5.5 Review and adjust the program

Perhaps most significantly, the legal standard for information security recognizes that security is a moving target. Businesses must constantly keep up with ever changing threats, risks, vulnerabilities, and security measures available to respond to them. It is a never-ending process. As a consequence, businesses must conduct periodic internal reviews to evaluate and adjust the information security program[28] in light of:

- The results of the testing and monitoring.
- Any material changes to the business or arrangements.
- Any changes in technology.
- Any changes in internal or external threats.
- Any environmental or operational changes.
- Any other circumstances that may have a material impact.[29]

In addition to periodic internal reviews, best practices and the developing legal standard may require that businesses obtain a periodic review and assessment (audit) by qualified independent third-party professionals using procedures and standards generally accepted in the profession. This is to certify that the security program meets or exceeds applicable requirements, and is operating with sufficient effectiveness to provide reasonable assurances that the security, confidentiality, and integrity of information is

---

[28] From Appendix, Microsoft Consent Decree at II, p. 4; Ziff Davis Assurance of Discontinuance, Para. 27(e) and (f), p. 7; Eli Lilly Decision at II.D, GLB Security Regulations, 12 CFR Part 30, Appendix B, Part III.E; HIPAA Security Regulations, 45 CFR Section 164.306(e) and 164.308(a)(8).

[29] GLB Security Regulations, 12 CFR Part 30 Appendix B, Part II.E; HIPAA Security Regulations, 45 CFR Section 164.308(a)(8); Microsoft Consent Decree at II, p. 4; Eli Lilly Decision at II.D.

protected.[30] It should then adjust the security program in light of the findings or recommendations that come from such reviews.[31]

5.6 Oversee third party service providers

Finally, in today's business environment it is important to recognize that companies often rely on third parties, such as outsource providers, to handle much of their data. When corporate data is in the possession and under the control of a third party, this presents special challenges for ensuring security.

Laws and regulations imposing information security obligations on businesses often expressly address requirements with respect to the use of third party outsource providers.[32] And first and foremost, they make clear that regardless of who performs the work, the legal obligation to provide the security itself remains with the company. As it is often said, "you can outsource the work, but not the responsibility." Thus, third party relationships should be subject to the same risk management, security, privacy, and other protection policies that would be expected if a business were conducting the activities directly.[33]

---

[30] Microsoft Consent Decree at III, p. 5.

[31] Ziff Davis Assurance of Discontinuance, Para. 27(h), p. 7.

[32] See e.g. US GLB Security Regulations, 12 CFR Part 30 Appendix B, Part II.D(2); HIPAA Security Regulations, 45 CFR Section 164.308(b)(1) and 164.314(a)(2); Belgium Act, Article 16(1); Denmark Act, Article 42(2); ED Data Protection Directive, Article 17; France Act, Article 38; Japan Act, Article 22; Netherlands Act, Article 14; Philippines Act, Section 8; Spain Act, Article 12; United Arab Emirates Act, Articles 15(3) and 16(3).

[33] See e.g. Office of the Comptroller of the Currency, Administrator of National Banks, OCC Bulletin 2001-47 on Third Party Relationships, November 21, 2001 (available at www.OCC.treas.gov/ftp/bulletin/2001-47.doc).

Generally, the developing legal standard for security imposes three basic requirements on businesses that outsource: (1) they must exercise due diligence in selecting service providers;[34] (2) they must contractually require outsource providers to implement appropriate security measures;[35] and (3) they must monitor the performance of the outsource providers.[36]

---

[34] See e.g. GLB Security Regulations, 12 CFR Part 30 Appendix B, Part II.D(1).
[35] See e.g. GLB Security Regulations, 12 CFR Part 30 Appendix B, Part II.D(2); HIPAA Security Regulations, 45 CFR Section 164.308(b)(1) and 164.314(a)(2).
[36] GLB Security Regulations, 12 CFR Part 30 Appendix B, Part II.D(3).

CHAPTER 6: SECURITY CONTROLS TO CONSIDER

As noted in Section 4.1, many security laws and regulations merely require "reasonable" or "appropriate" security, without any specification as to what security controls are required. Other security laws and regulations, however, do specify a variety of security controls that must be addressed by a company's security program. But in almost all cases they list only the *categories* of security controls that must be addressed, without requiring that any specific security controls or technologies be implemented. As explained in Section 5.3, the company selects which security controls to implement (so as to be legally compliant) by reference to the risk assessment.

This chapter identifies and explains the *categories* of security controls most often cited in security laws and regulations. No single law or regulation expressly requires that all of these controls be addressed, but when all of the security laws and regulations are viewed as a group, the categories of controls identified here emerge as the set most likely to be required for global legal compliance.

Moreover, given the process-oriented nature of the legal standard for security (discussed in Chapter 4), there is a good possibility that a requirement to at least consider many of these controls will be read into security laws and regulations that do not expressly identify them. Thus, if some of these categories of controls are not addressed by a company's security program, a court or regulator may well conclude that the company has not satisfied its obligation to implement "reasonable" or "appropriate" security under the applicable law.

It is important to stress, however, that while the law will likely require that a company's security program addresses the controls listed here (even if they are not expressly mentioned in the applicable law or regulation), the law does not typically specify how that must be done. Moreover, if the company "considers" a security control, but finds it to be unnecessary in light of its own risk assessment, that may well be sufficient, so long as the fact that the control was considered, and the reasons for not adopting it, are adequately documented.

Even where a particular control category is deemed to be relevant, the manner in which it is addressed, and the approach or technology used, is typically up to the company. The law does not require companies to implement security controls in a particular way or use a particular technology. As expressly stated in the HIPAA security regulations, for example, companies "may use any security measures" reasonably designed to achieve the objectives specified in the regulations.[1]

The organization of the categories of security controls listed below is subject to many different approaches. Thus, some of the labels used here may not be used in other listings, or certain controls may be grouped under different headings. With respect to each control, a footnote reference to the description of the control category in applicable ISO and NIST standards is also included.

---

[1] HIPAA Security Regulations, 45 CFR Section 164.306(b)(1).

6: Security Controls to Consider

6.1 Physical security controls

6.1.1 Facility and equipment

Security regulations frequently require companies to protect the security of their facility, their physical equipment comprising the information system, and the physical media on which their information is stored against destruction, loss, or damage.[2] Such physical and environmental security controls typically fall into three general categories: physical access restrictions, protections against technological failures, and protection against environmental threats.[3]

Physical access controls are common. Security laws and regulations frequently require that the company implement security measures and procedures to prevent unauthorized persons from gaining physical access to the buildings, computer facilities, and records storage facilities containing the equipment and the media.[4] This includes restricting physical access to the premises where the information systems used for processing personal data are located,[5] and restricting physical access to the data processing equipment used for storing, accessing, and processing the data.[6] It may also include controlling physical access to system devices that display information in order to prevent

---

[2] HIPAA Security Regulations, 45 CFR Section 164.310.
[3] See e.g. ISO27002, Section 9 (Physical and Environmental Security) pp. 29-36; NIST Special Publication 800-53, *Recommended Security Controls for Federal Information Systems* (February 2005) pp. 76-81 (Physical and Environment Protection).
[4] GLB Security Regulations, 12 CFR Part 30 Appendix B, Part III.C; HIPAA Security Regulations, 45 CFR Section 164.310(a).
[5] Italy Act, Annex B, Section 19.4; Poland – Ordinance, Attachment A (Basic Security Measures) § I.1; Portugal Act, Article 15(1)(a).
[6] Estonia Act, Section 19(2); Italy Act, Annex B, Section 19.4.

unauthorized individuals from observing the display output, for example, procedures that govern the use and security of physical workstations may be useful.[7]

Controls to protect against technological failures are often important. This may include, for example, requirements to implement controls such as providing short-term uninterruptible power supply for emergency power, automatic emergency lighting systems, and temperature and humidity controls.[8] Requirements to protect equipment and media from water damage resulting from broken plumbing lines and other sources of water leakage may also be included.[9]

Environmental controls are also important. This includes, for example, controls to protect against environmental incidents, such as deploying fire suppression and detection systems.[10]

6.1.2 Media

Media protection security controls are often necessary in order to ensure that security is not compromised through the improper handling of storage media. Thus, security laws and regulations may require companies to implement security controls to prevent data media from being read,

---

[7] HIPAA Security Regulations, 45 CFR Sections 164.310(b) and (c).
[8] GLB Security Regulations, 12 CFR Part 30 Appendix B, Part III.C [technological failures].
[9] GLB Security Regulations, 12 CFR Part 30 Appendix B, Part III.C.
[10] GLB Security Regulations, 12 CFR Part 30 Appendix B, Part III.C.

copied, altered or removed by unauthorized persons.[11] Security controls relevant here include the following:[12]

- Media access – ensuring that only authorized users have access to information in printed form or to the digital media on which it is stored.
- Media storage – securely storing removable media in a manner designed to prevent unauthorized access and processing.[13]
- Media transport – ensuring that devices and media that are taken outside of the premises are secured in a manner that guarantees the confidentiality and integrity of the data,[14] and ensuring that all media accessible to repair personnel have all data removed in a way that makes the recovery of data impossible or are repaired under appropriate supervision.[15]
- Media destruction and disposal – ensuring that the deletion/destruction of the data and/or the media on which it resides is secure (i.e. to ensure that the data cannot be recreated),[16] and procedures for removal from media before re-use of the media.[17]

The issue of media destruction and disposal has been the subject of several new laws and regulations. These laws typically do not require the destruction of data, but seek to

---

[11] Estonia Act, Section 19(2); Portugal Act, Article 15(1)(b).
[12] See e.g. ISO27002, Section 10.7 (Media Handling) pp. 46-48; NIST Special Publication 800-53, *Recommended Security Controls for Federal Information Systems* (February 2005) pp. 73-75 (Media Protection).
[13] Italy Act, Annex B, Section 21.
[14] HIPAA Security Regulations, 45 CFR Section 164.310(d); Poland Ordinance, Attachment Part B (Medium Security Measures), § IX.
[15] Poland – Ordinance, Attachment A (Basic Security Measures) § VI.
[16] HIPAA Security Regulations, 45 CFR Section 164.310(d)(2)(i).
[17] HIPAA Security Regulations, 45 CFR Section 164.310(d)(2)(ii).

regulate the manner of destruction when companies decide to do so. They require companies to properly dispose of personal information by taking reasonable measures to protect against unauthorized access to, or use of, the information in connection with its disposal.

With respect to information in paper form, this typically requires implementing policies and procedures that necessitate the burning, pulverizing, or shredding of papers containing personal information so that the information cannot be read or reconstructed. With respect to electronic information, such regulations typically require implementing policies and procedures that oblige the destruction or erasure of electronic media containing consumer personal information so that the information cannot practicably be read or reconstructed.[18]

In the US, both the banking regulators and the securities regulators have adopted rules regarding security requirements for the destruction of personal data. Similarly, at the state level, many states have adopted comparable requirements.[19] Several other countries have also adopted requirements to destroy removable media containing personal data no longer used, or alternatively to render personal data on such removable media unintelligible and not capable of reconstruction by any technical means before re-use of such removable media is allowed.[20]

---

[18] See e.g. 16 CFR Section 682.3 and statutes listed in the Appendix.
[19] See list in Appendix.
[20] See e.g. Italy Act, Annex B, Section 22; Poland – Ordinance, Attachment A (Basic Security Measures) § VI.

6.2 Technical security controls

6.2.1 Access controls

Access controls include security measures to: (1) prevent unauthorized persons from gaining access to systems and data, and (2) appropriately limit and control the scope of access granted to any authorized person[21] (*see Section 1.2*).

Numerous laws and regulations require companies to implement security measures and procedures to control access to their information systems and data.[22] This includes procedures to determine who is authorized to access the system;[23] procedures for granting and controlling access to the system in accordance with applicable policy,[24] such as authentication procedures (e.g. user ID and passwords, as discussed in the next section); procedures for regularly verifying that the relevant authorization profiles still apply;[25] and procedures for terminating access when it is no longer authorized (e.g. a person's employment has terminated or their role within the company has changed).[26]

Other laws impose requirements that data cannot be read, copied, modified or removed without authorization,[27] and

---

[21] See e.g. ISO27002, Section 11 (Access Control) pp. 60-76; NIST Special Publication 800-53, *Recommended Security Controls for Federal Information Systems* (February 2005) pp. 40-47 (Access Control).

[22] See e.g. Estonia Act, Section 19(2)(2); Poland – Ordinance, Attachment A (Basic Security Measures) § II.1.

[23] HIPAA Security Regulations, 45 CFR Section 164.308(a)(3)(ii); GLB Security Regulations, 12 CFR Part 30 Appendix B, Part III.C.

[24] HIPAA Security Regulations, 45 CFR Section 164.308(a)(4) and 164.312(a).

[25] Italy Act, Annex B, Section 14.

[26] HIPAA Security Regulations, 45 CFR Section 164.308(a)(3)(ii)(C).

[27] See e.g. German Federal Data Protection Act, Annex (to the first sentence of Section 9 of this Act), Section 3; Poland – Ordinance, Attachment A (Basic Security Measures) § II.1.

that measures be taken to prevent unauthorized persons from gaining access to the information systems where personal data are processed or used.[28]

Regulations often require companies to implement security measures and procedures to establish an appropriate level of authorization for persons entitled to access the personal data. This includes measures and procedures to ensure that personnel will only have access to the data and resources they need to perform their duties, and that are only able to access the data within the scope and to the extent covered by their respective access permission.[29] Procedures to prevent information systems from being used without (or in excess of) authorization are also required in some cases.[30]

Some regulations also address the authorization process itself. Specifically, they require that the company ensure that only authorized personnel may (i) create, modify or cancel the rights of access of other employees, agents and contractors, and (ii) access the hardware and computer components where the authorization databases are processed.[31]

---

[28] See e.g. German Federal Data Protection Act, Annex (to the first sentence of Section 9 of this Act), Section 1; Italy Act, Section 34(e) and Annex B, Sections 1 – 13; Portugal Act, Article 15(1)(d).

[29] Belgium Act, Art. 16(2)(2); Estonia Act, Sections 19(2)(2) and 19(2)(4); German Federal Data Protection Act, Annex (to the first sentence of Section 9 of this Act), Section 1; Italy Act, Section 34(c) and Annex B, Sections 12 and 13; Poland – Ordinance, Section § 5.1; Slovakia Act, Section 16(6)(b) and (c); Spain Royal Decree 1720/2007, Article 91 (Basic-level security measures).

[30] German Federal Data Protection Act, Annex (to the first sentence of Section 9 of this Act), Section 2; Italy Act, Section 34 and Annex B, Sections 1 – 13; Portugal Act, Article 15(1)(e); Spain Royal Decree 1720/2007, Article 91 (Basic-level security measures).

[31] Spain Royal Decree 1720/2007, Articles 91 and 99 (Basic-level and medium-level security measures).

6.2.2 *Identification and authentication*

Controlling access to systems and data requires determining whether a person (or device) seeking access is someone previously authorized to have access. This requires properly authenticating the identity of persons and devices seeking access to verify that they are authorized. Thus, it is important to implement security procedures to identify those persons and devices authorized to access the system and its data, and to authenticate the identity of persons and devices claiming to have such authorization when seeking online access.[32]

Such a requirement is expressly addressed, for example, in most US information security laws and regulations, including HIPAA,[33] GLB,[34] the Homeland Security Act,[35] FDA regulations,[36] and state information security laws.[37] Likewise, in April 2007 the Federal Communications Commission (FCC) issued an Order that imposes specific authentication requirements on telephone and wireless carriers to protect personal telephone records from unauthorized disclosure.[38] Numerous other country laws

---

[32] See e.g. ISO27002, Section 11 (Access Control) pp. 60-76; NIST Special Publication 800-53, *Recommended Security Controls for Federal Information Systems* (February 2005) pp. 65-67 (Identification and Authentication).

[33] HIPAA Security Regulations, 45 CFR § 164.312(d).

[34] GLBA Security Regulations, 12 CFR Part 30 Appendix B, Part III.C(1)(a).

[35] Homeland Security Act of 2002 § 1001(b), amending 44 USC § 3532(b)(1)(D), and § 301(b)(1) amending 44 USC § 3542(b)(1) ("'information security' means protecting information and information systems from unauthorized access, ...").

[36] Food and Drug Administration regulations, 21 CFR Part 11.

[37] See e.g. Cal. Civil Code § 1798.81.5(b).

[38] See FCC Order re Pretexting, 2 April 2007 – In the Matter of Implementation of the Telecommunications Act of 1996: Telecommunications Carriers' Use of Customer Proprietary Network Information and Other Customer Information IP-Enabled Services, CC Docket No. 96-115, WC Docket No. 04-36, 2 April 2007, Paragraphs 13-25; available at http://hraunfoss.fcc.gov/edocs_public/attachmatch/FCC-07-22A1.pdf (hereinafter "FCC Pretexting Order").

impose similar requirements.[39]   And in a recent case involving identity theft, a court found that there was a common law duty to authenticate the identity of a person submitting a credit card application.[40]

In all cases, the key issue is not whether authentication is required, but rather, what form of authentication is legally appropriate.   Security laws and regulations take varying approaches.

Some, for example, provide that authentication credentials must be assigned to each authorized user, and that such authentication credentials shall consist of: a user ID for each user, associated with a secret password known only to such person;[41] or an authentication device to be used and held exclusively by the user, and associated with either a user ID or a password, or else a biometric feature that relates to the user and is associated with either a user ID or a password.[42]

Historically, the standard approach to authentication of identity has been to use a user ID and password. And some regulations impose somewhat detailed rules where the authentication credentials consist of a user ID and password. These may include, for example, requirements that the company have procedures and mechanisms in place to:

---

[39] See e.g. Italy Act, Section 34(a) and (b) and Annex B, Sections 1 - 13; Poland – Ordinance, Section § 5.2 and Attachment A (Basic Security Measures) § II.2; Spain Royal Decree 1720/2007, Articles 93 and 98 (Basic-level and medium-level security measures).

[40] *Wolfe v. MBNA America Bank*, 485 F.Supp.2d 874, 882 (W.D. Tenn. 2007).

[41] Italy Act, Annex B, Section 2; Poland Ordinance, Attachment A (Basic Security Measures) § II.2.

[42] Italy Act, Annex B, Section 2; Poland Ordinance, Attachment A (Basic Security Measures) § II.2.

- specify the assignment, distribution, storage and frequency of changes of passwords;[43]
- ensure that passwords consist of at least 8 characters made up of small and large letters, numbers and special symbols;[44]
- ensure that passwords do not contain any item that can be easily related to the user;[45]
- ensure that passwords are modified by each user when first used, as well as at least once every 30 days[46] thereafter;
- ensure that the user ID of a user who is no longer authorized to perform data processing cannot be allocated to a different person;[47]
- de-activate the user ID and password if: (1) they have not been used for at least six months, except for those that have been authorized exclusively for technical management purposes,[48] or (2) the user is disqualified from accessing personal data;[49]
- instruct users to the effect that electronic equipment should not be left unattended and accessible during processing sessions;[50] and
- ensure that data or electronic equipment are available in case the user is either absent or unavailable for a long

---

[43] Spain Royal Decree 1720/2007, Article 93 (Basic-level security measures).
[44] Poland – Ordinance, Attachment Part B (Medium Security Measures), § VIII.
[45] Italy Act, Annex B, Section 5.
[46] Italy Act, Annex B, Section 5 (every 6 months); Poland – Ordinance, Attachment A (Basic Security Measures) § IV.2.
[47] Italy Act, Annex B, Section 6; Poland – Ordinance, Attachment A (Basic Security Measures) § IV.1.
[48] Italy Act, Annex B, Section 7.
[49] Italy Act, Annex B, Section 8.
[50] Italy Act, Annex B, Section 9.

time and it is indispensable to carry out certain activities without further delay, exclusively for purposes related to information system or personal data operation and security. In this case, copies of the credentials shall be kept in such a way as to ensure their confidentiality by specifying, in writing, the entities in charge of keeping such credentials.[51]

But based on recent developments, the use of user ID and password alone for authentication may no longer be *legally* adequate in all cases. In the US, regulators in the financial sector were the first to formally state that reliance solely on a user ID and password – so-called single-factor authentication – is considered "to be *inadequate*" at least in the case of high-risk transactions.

This new view of online authentication came in a guidance document issued by the FFIEC[52] in late 2005 titled "Authentication in an Internet Banking Environment" (FFIEC Guidance).[53] While the FFIEC Guidance applies to the financial sector, it is clearly in line with the developing law of security, and thus may well become legal best practice for all companies, especially where access to

---

[51] Italy Act, Annex B, Section 10.

[52] Federal Financial Institutions Examinations Council. The FFIEC is a formal US interagency government regulatory body empowered to prescribe uniform principles, standards, and report forms for the federal examination of US financial institutions by the Board of Governors of the Federal Reserve System (FRB), the Federal Deposit Insurance Corporation (FDIC), the National Credit Union Administration (NCUA), the Office of the Comptroller of the Currency (OCC), and the Office of Thrift Supervision (OTS), and to make recommendations to promote uniformity in the supervision of financial institutions. See www.ffiec.gov.

[53] FFIEC, *Authentication in an Internet Banking Environment*, 12 October 2005 (FFIEC Guidance), available at http://www.ffiec.gov/pdf/authentication_guidance.pdf. This was later supplemented by an FAQ titled "Frequently Asked Questions on FFIEC Guidance on Authentication in an Internet Banking Environment," 8 August 2006, available at http://www.ncua.gov/letters/2006/CU/06-CU-13_encl.pdf.

sensitive personal information is involved. Other countries, such as Singapore, have also adopted similar requirements.[54]

6.2.3 System and services acquisition controls

Acquisition of new systems and/or software for internal use, as well as acquisition of outsourced services that will access or process company data presents significant security risks.[55] Accordingly, security laws and regulations often require a company to adopt appropriate security policies and procedures to address system and services acquisition. Such controls should include the following:

For internal system acquisitions, this should include: (1) imposing appropriate security requirements and/or security specifications in information system acquisition contracts; (2) properly designing and implementing information systems using appropriate security engineering principles; and (3) properly testing and evaluating the security characteristics of such systems.

For outsourced services, most security regulations require companies to ensure that the third party providers of information system services employ adequate security controls in accordance with applicable laws, and to monitor compliance (*see Section 5.6*).

---

[54] Monetary Authority of Singapore, Circular No. SRD TR 02/2005, 25 November 2005.
[55] See e.g. ISO27002, Section 12 (Information Systems Acquisition, Development and Maintenance) pp. 77-89; ISO27002, Section 10.2 (Third Party Service Delivery Management) pp. 39-40; NIST Special Publication 800-53, *Recommended Security Controls for Federal Information Systems* (February 2005) pp. 89-92 (System and Services Acquisition).

6.2.4 System configuration and change management controls

Configuration controls address the security of the configuration of the various hardware and software components comprising the information system on which the data is used or stored.[56] This generally has two high-level components.

First, the company should identify and maintain records on the devices and software that comprise its information system,[57] and verify that the system and software configuration are appropriate from a security perspective.

Second, it should establish procedures to control any changes to the configuration to ensure that system modifications are consistent with the company's security program.[58] This includes, for example, protecting personal data in the event of changes to, movement of, or replacement of any hardware, computer component, software, or information related to the processing of personal data.[59]

6.2.5 System and information integrity

It is important to implement appropriate security controls to protect the integrity of the system and the information it contains. Such controls generally include checking data

---

[56] See e.g. ISO27002, Section 10.1.2 (Change Management) p. 37; NIST Special Publication 800-53, *Recommended Security Controls for Federal Information Systems* (February 2005) pp. 57-59 (Configuration Management).
[57] Estonia Act, Section 19(3).
[58] GLB Security Regulations, 12 CFR Part 30 Appendix B, Part III.C;
[59] Spain Royal Decree 1720/2007, Articles 91, 92, 94 and 101 (Basic-level and high-level security measures).

input validity and accuracy, data error handling, malicious code protection, intrusion detection tools, and procedures to verify software integrity.[60]

Various security regulations expressly require controls to address system and data integrity, including the following:

- *System integrity*: software integrity procedures to detect and protect against unauthorized changes to software, and to ensure that system modifications are consistent with the company's security program.[61]

- *Data integrity*: procedures and measures to protect information from unauthorized access, alteration, disclosure, or destruction during storage;[62] to ensure data integrity,[63] and to prevent the unauthorized or erroneous recording, alteration or erasure of personal data.[64]

- *Malicious code protection*: procedures for preventing, detecting, and reporting malicious software (e.g. virus software, Trojan horses, etc.),[65] and protecting the data against the effects of viruses, Trojan horses, worms, and other forms of malware.[66]

---

[60] See e.g. ISO27002, Section 10.4 (Protection Against Malicious and Mobile Code) pp. 42-43; NIST Special Publication 800-53, *Recommended Security Controls for Federal Information Systems* (February 2005) pp. 100-104 (System and Information Integrity).

[61] GLB Security Regulations, 12 CFR Part 30 Appendix B, Part III.C; Ziff Davis Assurance of Discontinuance, Para. 25, p. 6.

[62] See e.g. US – GLB Security Regulations, 12 CFR Part 30 Appendix B, Part III.C; HIPAA Security Regulations, 45 CFR Sections 164.312(c) and (e); Estonia Act, Section 19(2)(3); Portugal Act, Article 15(1)(c).

[63] Estonia Act, Section 19(1); Italy Act, Annex B, Section 19.4.

[64] Estonia Act, Section 19(2)(3).

[65] HIPAA Security Regulations, 45 CFR Section 164.308(a)(5)(ii)(B).

[66] Italy Act, Annex B, Section 16; Poland – Ordinance, Section 5.6 and Attachment A (Basic Security Measures) § III.1.

- *Intrusion detection*: tools, techniques and procedures to monitor log-in attempts and report discrepancies;[67] measures to detect actual and attempted attacks on or intrusions into company information systems;[68] and provide identification of unauthorized users. Ensure that personal data is protected against the risk of intrusion[69] including by the installation of physical or logic based safety systems providing protection against unauthorized access.[70] This might include, for example, limiting the number of unsuccessful attempts that are made to enter the information system or access the personal data.[71]

6.2.6 Data communications protection

It is important to implement appropriate controls to protect the confidentiality and integrity of data in the process of transfer or transmission.[72] This applies both to the transfer of data via hardware devices, such as laptops and USB drives, as well as to the transmission of data electronically, such as via the Internet.

This requirement is raised in several regulations, which address this concern in a variety of ways. Perhaps the most common approach is to require procedures designed to ensure that the data cannot be read, copied, modified,

---

[67] HIPAA Security Regulations, 45 CFR Section 164.308(a)(5)(ii)(C).

[68] GLB Security Regulations, 12 CFR Part 30 Appendix B, Part III.C; Ziff Davis Assurance of Discontinuance, Para. 24(d), p. 5 and Para. 25, p. 6.

[69] Italy Act, Annex B, Sections 16 and 20.

[70] Poland – Ordinance, Attachment Part C (High Security Measures), § XII.

[71] Spain Royal Decree 1720/2007, Article 98 (Medium-level security measures).

[72] See e.g. ISO27002, Section 10.8 (Exchange of Information) pp. 48-52; ISO27002, Section 10.8 (Electronic Commerce Services) pp. 53-55; NIST Special Publication 800-53, *Recommended Security Controls for Federal Information Systems* (February 2005) pp. 93-99 (System and Communications Protection).

disclosed, deleted, or otherwise unlawfully processed by unauthorized persons before it is allowed to leave the company.[73] Some regulations focus on laptops, and require special precautions when transporting, storing and using the equipment outside of the company premises, including such measures as encryption of the processed personal data.[74] Others focus on Internet communications, and require encryption of such communications.[75]

Some regulations also focus on requirements for procedures to ensure that no personal data is moved outside the premises without authorization of the company.[76] Others focus on the use of methods by which it is possible to check and establish when and to whom sensitive data is transferred by means of data transmission facilities.[77]

---

[73] See e.g. US – GLB Security Regulations, 12 CFR Part 30 Appendix B, Part III.C and HIPAA Security Regulations, 45 CFR Sections 164.312(c) and (e); Estonia Act, Section 19(2)(6); Hungary Act, Article 10(2); Ireland Act, Section 2-(1)(d); Italy Act, Annex B, Section 19.7; Poland – Ordinance, Attachment Part C (High Security Measures), § XIII; Portugal Act, Article 15(1)(h); Portugal Act, Article 15(4); Spain Royal Decree 1720/2007, Article 101 (High-level security measures).

[74] Poland – Ordinance, Attachment A (Basic Security Measures) § V.

[75] See e.g. US Maryland and Nevada Social Security Number laws; Portugal Act, Article 15(4) (requiring encryption of the transmission of personal data over a public network where the transmission may jeopardize the fundamental rights, freedoms and guarantees of the data subjects).

[76] See e.g. Spain Royal Decree 1720/2007, Article 92 (Basic-level security measures).

[77] Estonia Act, Section 19(2)(5); German Federal Data Protection Act, Annex (to the first sentence of Section 9 of this Act), Section 4; Portugal Act, Article 15(1)(f).

6.2.7 Maintenance

System hardware and software maintenance requirements raise a variety of information security concerns.[78] They normally fall into two general categories.

First, system maintenance is critical to ensure that the software is kept up-to-date so that others are not able to exploit newly-discovered vulnerabilities. In particular, this often requires procedures to identify, report, and correct information system flaws and potential vulnerability resulting from those flaws, such as by ensuring that newly released software security patches are identified, tested, and promptly installed.

Thus some regulations expressly require that the company implement security measures and procedures for the regular updating and patching of computer programs to eliminate vulnerabilities and remove flaws that could otherwise facilitate security breaches.[79] In one case in the US failure to promptly install security patches resulted in liability for a telecommunications company.[80]

Second, it is important that appropriate policies and procedures be in place to ensure that the process of doing hardware and software maintenance does not compromise security. For example, where it is necessary to remove system components or storage media from the facility for

---

[78] See e.g. ISO27002, Section 12 (Information Systems Acquisition, Development and Maintenance) pp. 77-89; NIST Special Publication 800-53, *Recommended Security Controls for Federal Information Systems* (February 2005) pp. 70-72 (Maintenance).
[79] Italy Act, Annex B, Section 17.
[80] *Inquiry Regarding the Entry of Verizon-Maine Into The InterLATA Telephone Market Pursuant To Section 271 of Telecommunication Act of 1996*, Docket No. 2000-849, Maine Public Utilities Commission, 2003 Me. PUC LEXIS 181, 30 April 2003; available at www.maine.gov/mpuc/orders/2000/2000-849o.htm.

repair, the company should have procedures in place to ensure that the receipt and removal of hardware and electronic media into and out of a facility does not compromise security.[81] This might include removing all information from media before it leaves the premises, and checking hardware and software security features after maintenance is performed to ensure that they are still functioning properly.[82]

Likewise, where maintenance is conducted remotely, the company should approve, control, and monitor remotely such activities to ensure that security is not compromised in the process. And of course, only authorized personnel should be allowed to perform such maintenance.

6.2.8 System activity monitoring and audit records

Information system and database events should be monitored and audit logs and accountability records should be maintained in order to track system use and activity to assist in the detection and investigation of potential security issues.[83] This includes, implementing security measures and procedures for monitoring access to sensitive data and for monitoring additions to, and alterations, deletions, and copying of, such data. Some regulations require, for example, that it be possible to determine when, by whom and which personal data were recorded, altered or erased.[84]

---

[81] HIPAA Security Regulations, 45 CFR Section 164.310(d).

[82] Poland – Ordinance, Attachment A (Basic Security Measures) § VI.

[83] See e.g. US – HIPAA Security Regulations, 45 CFR Section 164.312(b); Estonia Act, Section 19(2)(3); Poland – Ordinance, Sections § 7.1 – 7.3; Spain Royal Decree 1720/2007, Articles 97 and 103 (Medium and high-level security measures).

[84] Estonia Act, Section 19(2)(3); German Federal Data Protection Act, Annex (to the first sentence of Section 9 of this Act), Section 5; Portugal Act, Article 15(1)(g).

Based on its risk assessment, the company should decide which system events require auditing on a continuous basis, and which events require auditing in response to specific situations. Companies should also consider the content of: audit records; audit processing and storage procedures; audit monitoring, analysis, and reporting procedures; the protection of audit information; the retention of audit information; and establishing the auditing process in a manner such that it supports non-repudiation.[85]

For example, some regulations require monitoring of access to PCs, workstations or other units, indicating the specific equipment or machine accessing the information system or personal data, the date and time of access, the name of the user, the number of concurrent users, the kind of access, the files accessed and the kind of information processed, which personal data were recorded, copied, altered or erased, transmissions of data and name of the recipient, and acceptance or rejection of such access by the information system or personal data.[86]

---

[85] See e.g. ISO27002, Section 10.10 (Monitoring) pp. 55-59; NIST Special Publication 800-53, *Recommended Security Controls for Federal Information Systems* (February 2005) pp. 50-53 (Audit and Accountability).

[86] Estonia Act, Section 19(2)(3); Spain Royal Decree 1720/2007, Articles 97 and 103 (Medium and high-level security measures).

6.3 Administrative security controls

6.3.1 Personnel security

Personnel security controls are designed to address risks associated with individuals.[87] Thus, these controls apply not only to employees, but also to third-party personnel employed by contractors, technology service providers, and outsourced application providers. The focus is on the risks presented by persons who are not properly trained or qualified for the job, persons who may be dishonest, and persons who may be otherwise motivated to do inappropriate or destructive acts.

To address these concerns, security laws and regulations frequently require companies to verify that their employees, agents and contractors have the technical expertise and personal integrity required for their position,[88] and take steps to ensure the reliability of employees who have access to the information system or sensitive corporate data.[89] They may also require screening individuals requiring access to information before authorizing access to ensure that granting them access is appropriate, including, where appropriate, requiring background checks for employees with access to sensitive information.[90]

Security regulations may require clearly specifying the obligations of all employees, agents, and contractors

---

[87] See e.g. ISO27002, Section 8 (Human Resources Security) pp. 23-28; NIST Special Publication 800-53, *Recommended Security Controls for Federal Information Systems* (February 2005) pp. 84-86 (Personnel Security).

[88] Greece Act, Article 10(2).

[89] UK, Schedule 1, Part II, Seventh Principle, Section 10.

[90] GLB Security Regulations, 12 CFR Part 30 Appendix B, Part III.C.

entrusted with access to sensitive data.[91] They may also focus on work processes, recommending consideration of dual control procedures, segregation of duties, and other personnel management procedures for employees with responsibility for or access to information to be protected.[92] Some regulations require appropriate supervision of workforce members who work with sensitive information or in locations where it might be accessed.[93] Controls to prevent employees from providing information to unauthorized individuals who may seek to obtain this information through fraudulent means are also important.[94]

Sanctions are also an important part of personnel controls. Thus, some regulations expressly require that companies employ a formal sanctions process for personnel failing to comply with established security policies and procedures.[95]

Policies relating to personnel termination are also a critical component. Personnel security controls must address issues such as prompt termination of system access, exit interviews, insuring the return of all company property, (e.g. keys, ID cards, building passes), and ensuring that appropriate personnel have access to official records created by the terminated employee that are stored on information systems.[96]

---

[91] Spain Royal Decree 1720/2007, Article 89 (Basic-level security measures).
[92] GLB Security Regulations, 12 CFR Part 30 Appendix B, Part III.C.
[93] HIPAA Security Regulations, 45 CFR Section 164.308(a)(3)(ii)(A).
[94] GLB Security Regulations, 12 CFR Part 30 Appendix B, Part III.C.
[95] See e.g. US – GLB Security Regulations, 12 CFR Part 30 Appendix B, Part III.C and HIPAA Security Regulations, 45 CFR Section 164.308(a)(1)(ii)(C).
[96] HIPAA Security Regulations, 45 CFR Section 164.308(a)(3)(ii)(C).

6.3.2 *Employee awareness and training*

Training and education for employees is a critical component of any security program. It is the primary vehicle for disseminating security information that employees need to do their jobs, and for providing them with the information and tools needed to protect the company's vital information resources.

Numerous audit reports, studies, and surveys confirm that people are often the weakest link in the security chain. Even the very best physical, technical, and administrative security measures are of little value if employees do not understand their roles and responsibilities with respect to security. For example, installing heavy duty doors with state of the art locks (whether of the physical or virtual variety) will not provide the intended protection if the employees authorized to have access leave the doors open and unlocked for unauthorized persons to pass through.

Thus, the legal standard for reasonable security mandates appropriate security awareness training and education for employees.[97] The goal is to ensure that all employees, agents, and contractors are aware of and comply with the relevant security measures implemented by the company to protect the data. A good example is the regulations issued under the US Computer Security Act, which require federal agencies to provide mandatory periodic training in computer security awareness and accepted computer security practice for all employees who are involved with

---

[97] See e.g. US – GLB Security Regulations, 12 CFR Part 30 Appendix B, Part III.C and HIPAA Security Regulations, 45 CFR Section 164.308(a)(5); Estonia Act, Section 20(3); Ireland Act, Section 2C(2); Italy Act, Annex B, Sections 4 and 19.6; Slovakia Act, Sections 17 and 19(3); Spain Royal Decree 1720/2007, Article 89 (Basic-level security measures).

the management, use, or operation of a federal computer system within or under the supervision of a federal agency.[98]

Employee security awareness and training is, in many cases, the only security control that can minimize the inherent risk that results from the people who use, manage, operate, and maintain information systems and networks. Thus, security education should be provided for all employees who are involved with the management, use, or operation of a computer system or who access information contained therein. This includes contractors as well as employees of the company.

Security education[99] begins with communication to employees of applicable security policies, procedures, standards, and guidelines, as well as the requirements of the laws applicable to their activities and the data they will be working with.[100] It also includes periodic training in computer security awareness and accepted computer security practices,[101] periodic security reminders, and

---

[98] See 5 CFR Part 930.301, which specifies requirements for an information systems security awareness training program.

[99] See e.g. ISO27002, Section 8.2.2 (Information Security Awareness, Education and Training) p. 26; NIST Special Publication 800-53, *Recommended Security Controls for Federal Information Systems* (February 2005) pp. 48-49 (Awareness and Training). Although developed for the US federal government, NIST Special Publication 800-50, *Building an Information Technology Security Awareness and Training Program*, provides high level guidelines that can help companies meet their information security awareness and training responsibilities. The publication identifies models for building and maintaining a comprehensive awareness and training program as part of an organization's information security program. A companion publication, NIST Special Publication 800-16, *Information Technology Security Training Requirements: A Role- and Performance-Based Model*, addresses a more tactical level and discusses the awareness-training-education continuum, role-based training, and course content considerations.

[100] Belgium Act, Art 16(2)(3).

[101] See e.g. FISMA, 44 USC Section 3544(b)(4); HIPAA Security Regulations, 45 CFR Section 164.308(a)(5)(i); Ziff Davis Assurance of Discontinuance, Para. 24(d), p. 5.

developing and maintaining relevant employee training materials, such as user education concerning virus protection, password management, and how to report discrepancies.

Each user should be versed in acceptable rules of behavior for the application before being allowed access to the system. Training should also inform the user on how to get help when having difficulty in using the system and procedures for reporting security incidents.

6.3.3 Contingency planning – backup and disaster recovery

Security laws and regulations often require that the company develop and implement a contingency plan for the information system and data.[102] Such a plan should be designed to ensure that the company is able to continue operations and that the data will be available in the event of an emergency. This includes not only environmental emergencies, such as fire, flood, hurricane and earthquake, but also other potential threats, such as equipment failure, denial of service attacks, or sabotage.

Such a contingency plan[103] should include system and data backup procedures, and a recovery plan that specifies the procedures to be followed in case of emergencies, such as

---

[102] See e.g. US – HIPAA Security Regulations, 45 CFR Section 164.308(a)(7); Italy Act, Annex B, Section 19.5; Slovakia Act, Article 16(6); Spain Royal Decree 1720/2007, Article 94 (Basic-level security measures).
[103] See e.g. ISO27002, Section 14 (Business Continuity Management) pp. 95-99; ISO27002, Section 10.5 (Back-up) pp. 44-45; NIST Special Publication 800-53, *Recommended Security Controls for Federal Information Systems* (February 2005) pp. 60-64 (Contingency Planning).

fire, vandalism, system failure and natural disasters.[104] This often requires provision of alternate secure storage site(s) to permit the storage of back-up information; alternate processing site(s) to facilitate the resumption of system operations for critical functions; alternate telecommunications services to support the information system; and entering into necessary agreements to establish the foregoing.[105] Back-up and retention procedures should also ensure that regular back-up copies are made and properly stored, and that they are properly deleted immediately after they cease to be of any use.[106]

It should also provide for appropriate mechanisms to allow the information system and the data to be recovered and reconstituted to its original state after disruption, failure, destruction or damage.[107]

The plan should also designate appropriate personnel and specify their roles, responsibilities, and activities associated with restoring the system after a disruption or a failure. Training for designated personnel in their contingency roles and responsibilities with respect to the information system is critical.

Testing of the contingency plan on a regular basis to determine its effectiveness and the company's readiness to

---

[104] See e.g. US – HIPAA Security Regulations, 45 CFR Section 164.308(a)(7); Spain Royal Decree 1720/2007, Article 94 (Basic-level security measures); Italy Act, Section 34(f) and Annex B, Section 19.5; Poland – Ordinance, Section § 5.4 and 5.5 and Attachment A (Basic Security Measures) § IV.3.

[105] See e.g. Spain Royal Decree 1720/2007, Article 102 (High-level security measures); Poland – Ordinance, Section § 5.2, and Attachment A (Basic Security Measures) § IV.4.

[106] See e.g. US – HIPAA Security Regulations, 45 CFR Section 164.308(a)(7); Italy Act, Annex B, Section 18; Poland – Ordinance, Attachment A (Basic Security Measures) § IV.4; Spain Royal Decree 1720/2007, Article 94 (Basic-level security measures).

[107] See e.g. Italy Act, Annex B, Section 23.

execute the plan is also important and often required by security regulations.[108] Likewise, regulations often require that the plan be reviewed on a regular basis and revised as necessary to address system or organizational changes or problems encountered during plan implementation, execution, or testing.[109]

6.3.4 Incident response plan

In addition to contingency planning, security laws often require companies to develop and implement incident response policies and procedures.[110] The goal is to provide a plan for taking responsive action (including notification, management, and response procedures) in the event the company suspects or detects that a security breach has occurred.[111] Such incident response policies and procedures typically address the following:[112]

- Incident reporting: procedures to ensure that appropriate persons within the organization are promptly notified of security breaches, and that (where appropriate) external authorities are notified as well.

- Incident handling and response: procedures to ensure that prompt action is taken to respond to the breach, including detection and analysis of the breach,

---

[108] See e.g. US – HIPAA Security Regulations, 45 CFR Section 164.308(a)(7); Spain Royal Decree 1720/2007, Article 94 (Basic-level security measures).
[109] HIPAA Security Regulations, 45 CFR Section 164.308(a)(7).
[110] See e.g. HIPAA Security Regulations, 45 CFR Section 164.308(a)(6); GLB Security Regulations, 12 CFR Part 30 Appendix B, Part III.C; Spain Royal Decree 1720/2007, Articles 90 and 100 (Basic and medium-level security measures).
[111] Spain Royal Decree 1720/2007, Article 90 (Basic-level security measures).
[112] See e.g. ISO27002, Section 13 (Information Security Incident Management) pp. 90-94; NIST Special Publication 800-53, *Recommended Security Controls for Federal Information Systems* (February 2005) pp. 68-69.

containment of the breach to stop further information compromise, eradication of the problem, recovery procedures, and procedures for working with outside experts and law enforcement where appropriate.

- Incident monitoring and recordkeeping: procedures to track and document each security incident on an ongoing basis, and to create appropriate records that include date and time of the incident, nature of the incident, impact of the incident, persons involved in responding to the incident, and procedures followed to resolve the incident.[113]

- Incident response assistance: policies for obtaining both inside and outside support and assistance for the handling and reporting of security incidents, and policies for notifying appropriate persons who may be potentially injured by the breach.

- Training: appropriate training for relevant personnel in their incident response roles and responsibilities.

- Testing: periodic testing of the incident response plan to determine its effectiveness and document the results.

6.4 Special rules for specific data elements

Some security statutes and regulations are also beginning to focus on specific data elements, and imposing specific obligations with respect to such data elements. Prime examples include so-called sensitive personal data, Social Security numbers, and credit card transaction data.

---

[113] Spain Royal Decree 1720/2007, Articles 90 and 100 (Basic and medium-level security measures).

6.4.1 Sensitive data

From its inception, the EU Data Protection Directive has required special treatment for particularly sensitive personal information. Specifically, the Directive prohibits "the processing of personal data revealing racial or ethnic origin, political opinions, religious or philosophical beliefs, trade-union membership, and the processing of data concerning health or sex life," unless certain exceptions apply.[114] Those exceptions include "explicit consent" by the data subject, and carrying out obligations under applicable employment laws.

But even with consent, processing such sensitive data, according to EU interpretation, requires that "special attention" be given to data security aspects to avoid risks of unauthorized disclosure. In particular, "*[a]ccess by unauthorized persons must be virtually impossible and prevented.*" [115] To that end, some EU country laws require that sensitive data be encrypted, logically separated from other data, or protected by other technical means that make such data illegible to any unauthorized third party.[116]

In the US a de facto category of sensitive information has been defined by the various state security breach notification laws (discussed in Chapter 8). These laws require special action (i.e. disclosure) in the event of a breach of security with respect to a subcategory of personal

---

[114] EU Data Protection Directive, Article 8.
[115] Article 29 Data Protection Working Party, Working Document on the processing of personal data relating to health in electronic health records (EHR), 00323/07/EN, WP 131, 15 February 2007, pp. 19-20; available at http://ec.europa.eu/justice_home/fsj/privacy/docs/wpdocs/2007/wp131_en.pdf (emphasis in original).
[116] Italy Act, Section 34(h), and Annex B, Sections 19.8 and 24; Portugal Act, Article 15(3); Spain Royal Decree 1720/2007, Article 101 (High-level security measures).

data generally considered to be sensitive because of its potential role in facilitating identity theft.

6.4.2 Social Security numbers (SSNs)

Separately, in the US, the security of Social Security numbers has also been the focus of numerous state laws enacted during the past few years (*see list in Appendix*). The scope of these laws range from restrictions on the manner in which Social Security numbers can be used, to express requirements for security with respect to the communication and/or storage of Social Security numbers. For example, several states have enacted laws that prohibit requiring an individual to transmit his or her Social Security number over the Internet unless the connection is secure or the individual's Social Security number is encrypted. The law in Maryland and Nevada goes further, and prohibits initiating any transmission of an individual's Social Security number over the Internet unless the connection is secure or the Social Security number is encrypted.[117]

The bottom line is that if a company wants to continue collecting, maintaining, and transferring data with SSNs, it will have to provide special treatment for the protection of that data (at least for the SSN portion), such as encryption, using secure communications media, controlling access, and adopting special security policies.

---

[117] Maryland Commercial Code, § 14-3402(a)(4); Nevada Rev. Stat. § 597.970.

6.4.3 Credit card data

For businesses that accept credit card transactions, the Payment Card Industry Data Security Standard (PCI Standard)[118] imposes significant security obligations with respect to credit card data captured as part of any credit card transaction. And at least one state (Minnesota) has also enacted a law imposing specific security obligations with respect to credit card data.[119]

---

[118] Available at www.pcisecuritystandards.org.
[119] Minnesota Plastic Card Security Act, Minn. Stat. Chapter 325E.64.

CHAPTER 7: THE ROLE OF STANDARDS

Technical standards, guidelines, best practices, and industry customs all play an important role in assisting companies as they work through the process of addressing their information security needs. But what role do they play, if any, in addressing legal compliance? In particular, given the many laws and regulations addressing security worldwide, are there any standards that a business can comply with and be assured of meeting all of its legal obligations (particularly on a global basis)?

7.1 Standards and industry customs

Standards, guidelines, best practices, and industry custom and usage all offer possible approaches to determining what level of security is appropriate in a given situation.

- *Standards* are perhaps the strongest and most detailed, and often result from formal standard-making processes. By one definition, for example, a standard is: "An agreement reached on products, practices, or operations and formally approved by nationally or internationally recognized industrial, professional, trade, or governmental bodies."[1] A standard represents (or seeks to represent) an established norm or requirement.

- *Guidelines or frameworks* are typically much less technical in character and instead speak in terms of

---

[1] Martin H. Weik, *Communications Standard Dictionary*, 3rd ed. Chapman & Hall, New York, N.Y., 1996.

principles, policies, and processes that ought to govern activities in order to achieve improved security.[2] By one measure, a standard is "Thou shall" while a guideline is a recommendation, more like "You should if your situation warrants."

- *Best practices* represent experience-based measures identified and compiled by people who seek to share their lessons-learned for the common good.[3]

- *Industry "custom and usage"* is simply the way things are done within an industry. It has been defined as "any practice or method of dealing having such regularity of observance in a place, vocation or trade as to justify an expectation that it will be observed with respect to the transaction in question."[4]

Many national and international organizations are working to define information security standards and best practices. These various standards provide benchmarks that companies and regulators can draw upon for the development of industry expectations and security practices. Some of the best known security standards include the following:[5]

7.1.1 ISO/IEC 27000 series standards

The ISO/IEC 27000 series standards are information security standards published jointly by the International

---

[2] Jody Westby, Ed. *International Guide to Cybersecurity*, American Bar Association (2004), p 159.
[3] Id, p. 159.
[4] US Uniform Commercial Code, Section 1-303(c) (2001).
[5] A list of technical security standards is available at
http://iso27001security.com/html/others.html.

Organization for Standardization (ISO) and the International Electrotechnical Commission (IEC).

ISO is the world's largest developer and publisher of International Standards, and is comprised of a network of the national standards institutes of 155 countries, with one member per country, and a Central Secretariat in Geneva, Switzerland, that coordinates the system.[6] The American National Standards Institute (ANSI) represents the United States.

The IEC, also based in Geneva, Switzerland coordinates, designs, and publishes international standards in fields related to electronics, including telecommunications. The electrotechnical standards organizations of each participating country make up its membership, with ANSI representing the United States.[7]

Two of the most important and often cited international information security standards in the ISO/IEC 27000 series are: ISO/IEC 27001:2005, *Information Technology – Security Techniques – Information Security Management Systems – Requirements* (Oct 2005) (hereinafter "ISO27001"); and ISO/IEC 27002:2005, *Information Technology – Security Techniques – Code of Practice for Information Security Management* (June 2005) (hereinafter "ISO27002"). ISO27001 was also formerly known as BS7799-2, and ISO27002 was formerly known as both BS7799-1 and ISO17799.

ISO27001 is designed to provide a model for establishing, implementing, operating, monitoring, reviewing,

---

[6] See www.iso.org/iso/home.htm.
[7] See www.iec.ch.

maintaining and improving what the standard refers to as an "Information Security Management System (ISMS)."[8] An ISMS is the framework to define, implement and monitor the security controls needed to protect the security of corporate information. It is essentially a suite of processes and systems for effectively managing information security, and is comparable to the "comprehensive information security plan" required by many security statutes and regulations (discussed in Chapters 4 and 5 above).

ISO27002 is a list of potential security controls that can be used in conjunction with ISO27001 as a checklist for developing security policies. Referring to ISO27002 by its prior designation, the Council for the European Union noted that: "The International Standard ISO17799 (Information technology – Code of Practice for Information Security Management) and similar national guidelines are becoming recognized practice for security management in private and public organizations."[9]

7.1.2 NIST standards and guidelines

Founded in 1901, the National Institute of Standards and Technology (NIST) is a non-regulatory federal agency within the US Department of Commerce.[10] NIST's mission is to promote US innovation and industrial competitiveness by advancing measurement science, standards, and

---

[8] ISO27001 § 0.1.

[9] Council of the European Union, Council Resolution of 28 January 2002 on a common approach and specific actions in the area of network and information security (2002/C 43/02), "whereas" clause number 11.

[10] www.nist.gov.

technology in ways that enhance economic security and improve quality of life.

NIST also has statutory responsibility to set security standards and guidelines for sensitive US federal systems, and these standards are often adopted and used by the private sector on a voluntary basis. In particular, the Computer Security Division[11] of NIST works to improve information systems security for consumers, industry, and government agencies, and develops standards, measurement methods, tests, and validation programs for information security. It provides services and guidance for vendors, government agencies, and computer users.

Those efforts include developing security standards known as the Federal Information Processing Standards, or FIPS Publications.[12] FIPS Publications are issued by NIST after approval by the Secretary of Commerce pursuant to the Information Technology Reform Act of 1996 and the Federal Information Security Management Act of 2002.

NIST also issues a series of security guidelines, known as Special Publications.[13] Special Publications in the 800 series present documents of general interest to the computer security community. The Special Publication 800 series was established in 1990 to provide a separate identity for information technology security publications.

---

[11] www.itl.nist.gov/div893/.
[12] http://csrc.nist.gov/publications/PubsFIPS.html.
[13] http://csrc.nist.gov/publications/PubsSPs.html.

7.1.3 COBIT framework

COBIT (Control Objectives for Information and related Technology) is a set of best practices (framework) for information technology management created by the Information Systems Audit and Control Association (ISACA),[14] and the IT Governance Institute (ITGI).[15] It seeks to provide an international set of generally accepted information technology control objectives for day-to-day use by business managers and auditors, and is designed to help them understand their IT systems and decide the level of security and control that is necessary to protect company assets through the development of an IT governance model.

7.1.4 Payment Card Industry Data Security Standard

The Payment Card Industry Data Security Standard (PCI Standard)[16] is a set of comprehensive requirements for enhancing credit and debit card payment account data security. It was developed by the PCI Security Standards Council,[17] which includes American Express, Discover Financial Services, JCB International, MasterCard Worldwide and Visa.

The PCI Standard includes requirements for security management, policies, procedures, network architecture, software design and other critical protective measures. This comprehensive standard is intended to proactively protect customer account data, and compliance by merchants that

---

[14] www.isaca.org/cobit.htm.
[15] See www.itgi.org. The IT Governance Institute is a research think tank that seeks to be the leading reference on IT governance for the global business community.
[16] https://www.pcisecuritystandards.org/security_standards/pci_dss.shtml.
[17] https://www.pcisecuritystandards.org/.

accept credit cards is contractually required by credit card processing contracts with acquiring banks.

7.1.5 ISF Standard of Good Practice for Information Security

The Standard of Good Practice for Information Security[18] addresses information security from a business perspective, and seeks to provide a practical basis for assessing an organization's information security arrangements. It consists of a comprehensive set of information security-specific controls, such as information risk analysis, security architecture, securing business applications, monitoring compliance, information classification, and information security strategy.

The Standard of Good Practice is published by the Information Security Forum (ISF),[19] an international, independent, not-for-profit organization dedicated to benchmarking and best practices in information security. The ISF is headquartered in London, England, but also has offices in New York City. Membership of the ISF is international and includes large organizations in transportation, financial services, chemical/pharmaceutical, manufacturing, government, retail, media, energy, telecommunications, transportation, professional services, and other sectors.

---

[18] https://www.isfsecuritystandard.com/SOGP07/index.htm.
[19] https://www.securityforum.org/index.htm.

7.2 The legal impact of standards

The general nature of most laws and regulations governing security, and the ever-growing number of such laws, has led many companies to ask a simple question: if we comply with a generally accepted technical standard, will we also satisfy all of our legal obligations?

Unfortunately, it is usually not that simple. As a general rule, adherence to a standard or prevailing industry practice may be *evidence* of compliance with a legal obligation, but whether it qualifies as compliance with the legal obligation is a matter for the trier of the facts to determine by the broader standard of what reasonable care and prudence demand under the same or similar circumstances.[20] In other words, compliance with a technical standard is not dispositive on the issue of liability.[21] Thus, as noted in ISO27001, "[c]ompliance with an International Standard does not in itself confer immunity from legal obligations."[22]

7.2.1 The relevance of industry custom

It is a well-established principle of tort law that industry custom is a relevant, but by no means conclusive, consideration in determining the standard of care against which an actor's conduct will be measured.[23] This is

---

[20] *Hunyadi v. The Stratfield Hotel, Inc.* 143 Conn. 77, 83; 119 A.2d 321; 1955 Conn. LEXIS 132 (1955). See also 2 Wigmore, *Evidence* (3d Ed.) p. 489.

[21] *Richardson v. Walsh Press & Die Company,* 1995 US Dist. LEXIS 11771 at *4 (S.D. NY, 1995); *Contini v. Hyundai Motor Co.* 865 F. Supp. 122, 123 (S.D.N.Y. 1994).

[22] ISO27001, p. 1.

[23] *See Darling v. Charleston Community Memorial Hospital,* 211 N.E.2d 253 (Ill. 1965), *cert. denied,* 383 US 946 (1966); see also *Texas & Pacific Railway Co. v. Behymer,* 189 US 468, 470 (per Just Oliver Wendell Holmes) ("What usually is done may be evidence of what ought to be done, but what ought to be done is fixed by a standard of reasonable

because, quite simply, courts often find that an industry custom may itself be inadequate.

Moreover, "if the only test is to be what has always been done, no one will ever have any great incentive to make any progress in the direction of safety."[24] As the leading authorities on torts have put it:

...customs and usages themselves are many and various; some are the result of careful thought and decision, while others arise from the kind of inadvertance, carelessness, indifference, cost-paring and corner-cutting that normally is associated with negligence . . . [But] Even an entire industry, by adopting such careless methods to save time, effort or money, cannot be permitted to set its own uncontrolled standard.[25]

This principle may have been best highlighted in the seminal *T.J. Hooper* case.[26] That case involved a claim based on the alleged failure to provide adequate security for a shipment of coal that was lost when an unexpected storm caused the sinking of the barge that was carrying it. The owner of the cargo argued that the cargo might not have been lost at sea had the tugboat towing the barge been equipped with a weather radio. Although the use of such a radio would have provided adequate warning of the storm, it was not customary in the industry at that time (1928) to install such radios in tugboats.

---

prudence, whether it is usually complied with or not"). See also, W. Page Keeton, et al., *Prosser and Keeton on the Law of Torts* § 33, 193 (5th ed. 1984).

[24] *Restatement (Second) of Torts* § 295A cmt. c (1965).

[25] W. Page Keeton, et al., *Prosser and Keeton on the Law of Torts* § 33, 194 (5th ed. 1984).

[26] In re *Eastern Transp. Co. v. Northern Barge Corp.* 60 F.2d 737 (2d Cir. 1932) (The T.J. Hooper case).

Nonetheless, the court rejected the argument that compliance with industry custom was a "safe harbor" from liability. The opinion stated:

> Indeed in most cases reasonable prudence is in fact common prudence, but strictly it is never its measure; a whole [industry] may have unduly lagged in the adoption of new and available devices. [An industry] never may set its own tests, however persuasive be its usages. Courts must in the end say what is required; there are precautions so imperative that even their universal disregard will not excuse their omission. [27]

Embedded in this principle that the industry itself cannot be permitted to set its own uncontrolled standards is the concept that some implicit minimum standard of care applies with respect to any given activity. In other words, industry customs most likely will only be deemed reasonable to the extent that they meet or exceed the minimum standards of reasonable care imposed by the courts, which are commensurate with the magnitude of the risks involved.

Thus, it seems clear that doing "what everyone else is doing" with respect to providing security is not necessarily the best road to legal compliance. In some cases, satisfying the legal requirements for reasonable security may require doing quite a bit more than what everyone else is doing.

In the context of information security, this principle is perhaps best illustrated by statements from the banking regulators in the US and Singapore with regard to the security requirements for authentication of persons seeking online access to their bank accounts. For many years, the industry custom has been to use a user ID and a password

---

[27] Id. p. 740.

to control access. But in late 2005, when phishing practices were beginning to have a serious impact, the banking regulators stated that this long-standing practice may no longer be *legally* adequate. In fact, they formally stated that, in their view reliance solely on a user ID and password – so-called single-factor authentication – was considered "to be *inadequate*" at least in the case of high-risk transactions.[28]

Shortly thereafter, the banking regulators in Singapore expressed a similar view.[29]   And in a Canadian case involving a laptop stolen from a school, a July 2008 ruling by the Privacy Commissioner of Newfoundland and Labrador reached a similar conclusion: "Use of network passwords alone to protect personal information does not constitute a 'reasonable security measure' as mandated by [the applicable privacy law]."[30]

As the foregoing makes clear, reliance on what everyone else is doing is not necessarily legally sufficient.

7.2.2 The relevance of standards

It also appears that courts generally view compliance with standards (as opposed to industry customs) in much the same light. As one court noted when deciding the question

---

[28] FFIEC, *Authentication in an Internet Banking Environment*, 12 October 2005, available at http://www.ffiec.gov/pdf/authentication_guidance.pdf.

[29] Monetary Authority of Singapore, *Two-Factor Authentication for Internet Banking*, Circular No. SRD TR 02/2005, 25 November 2005, available at www.mas.gov.sg/resource/legislation_guidelines/banks/circulars/Circular2FA25Nov05.pdf.

[30] *Eastern School District*, Report P-2008-002, Office of the Information and Privacy Commissioner, Newfoundland and Labrador, 23 July 2008, p. 27, available at www.oipc.gov.nl.ca/pdf/P-2008-002_Eastern%20School%20District.pdf.

of whether a company used reasonable care, "compliance with industry and statutory standards is *evidence* of the use of reasonable care, but it is not dispositive of that issue."[31]

In one case, for example, the court held that "proof that an electric company erected its lines at a height which complied with the minimum standards of the National Electrical Safety Code is a *factor which may be considered* by the jury on the issue of negligence, although not in itself an absolute defense."[32] But the converse may also be true. That is, failure to comply with such standards is evidence on the issue of negligence.[33]

The ability to satisfy legal obligations by compliance with private standards will also depend, in part, on the trustworthiness of the standard. As one court noted, the trustworthy requirement is satisfied when private organizations publishing the industry standards "are formed for the chief purpose of promoting safety, and the materials they publish generally represent not merely the opinion of one expert in a particular field but 'a consensus of opinion carrying the approval of a significant segment of an industry.'"[34]

7.3 ISO27001: Road to global legal compliance?

Compliance with industry standards is no guarantee of compliance with legal obligations. Yet, for companies seeking a shortcut to global compliance with security

---

[31] *Primrose Operating Co. v. Nat'l Am. Ins. Co.* 382 F.3d 546, 558 (5th Cir. 2004) (emphasis added).
[32] *McComish v. DeSoi*, 42 N.J. 274, 285 (N.J. 1964) (emphasis added).
[33] *Jorgensen v. Horton*, 206 N.W.2d 100, 103 (Iowa 1973).
[34] *Frazier v. Continental Oil Co.* 568 F.2d 378, 382 (5th Cir. 1978).

obligations, the ISO27001 standard is at least worth considering.

ISO27001 is a relatively new international standard that certainly has the appearance of a trustworthy standard, given the process by which it was prepared. Moreover, it offers two important advantages:

First, while ISO27001 is a technical standard for information security, it appears to be based on essentially the same premise as the legal standard for information security outlined in Chapters 4, 5 and 6 above. That is, it "adopts a *process approach* to establishing, implementing, operating, monitoring, reviewing, maintaining, and improving an organization's IMIS."[35] And it includes all of the requirements of the legal standard – i.e. compliance with the ISO27001 standard requires companies to identify their information assets,[36] conduct risk assessments,[37] select responsive security controls,[38] implement and operate their ISMS,[39] monitor and review their ISMS,[40] maintain and improve their ISMS,[41] and manage security of third parties.[42]

Thus, it can be argued that the adoption of ISO27001 by two international standards groups comprised of representatives from most countries (i.e. ISO and IEC), represents at least a tacit endorsement of the legal standard for security at an international level. Moreover, although

---

[35] ISO27001, § 0.2 (emphasis added).
[36] ISO27001, § 4.2.1.
[37] Id.
[38] Id.
[39] ISO27001, § 4.2.2.
[40] ISO27001, §§ 4.2.3 and 6.
[41] ISO27001, §§ 4.2.4 and 8.
[42] ISO27001, § A.10.2.

compliance with the ISO27001 standard does not guarantee legal compliance (e.g. it is not a safe harbor),[43] it may offer companies a good starting point on the road to addressing international legal requirements for security.

Second, ISO27001 is an auditable standard. That is, compliance with the standard can be certified by a third party qualified to do ISO27001 audits.

ISO27001 provides a model for an information security management system (ISMS), which is, in essence, similar to the concept of a comprehensive information security program as defined in many security statutes and regulations. And it adopts a process approach[44] that is very similar to the approach for the legal standard for security outlined in Chapters 4, 5 and 6 above. In fact, the ISO27001 process approach includes all of the elements that appear in the various legal requirements, although it organizes them somewhat differently.

Like the legally-required process for developing an information security program, "the ISMS is designed to ensure the selection of adequate and proportionate security controls that protect information assets and give confidence to interested parties."[45]

ISO27001 uses what it calls a "plan-do-check-act" (PDCA) model for purposes of developing an ISMS.[46] As it relates to the legal standard, the PDCA model may be summarized as follows:

---

[43] ISO27001 itself specifically states that "Compliance with an International Standard does not in itself confer immunity from legal obligations." p. 1.
[44] ISO27001, § 0.2.
[45] ISO27001, § 1.1.
[46] ISO27001, § 0.2.

Plan (establish the ISMS): The "plan" element of the ISO27001 process is, in essence, the first two elements of the legal program outlined in Sections 5.1 and 5.2 above (i.e. identify information assets and conduct risk assessments). While it includes more detail in terms of how to initiate and implement the process, the "plan" element of the ISO27001 process essentially incorporates requirements that the company identify its information assets (*see Section 5.1*) and that it conduct an appropriate risk assessment to identify, analyze, and evaluate the applicable risks, and to identify and evaluate options for the treatment of those risks (*see Section 5.2*).[47]

The "plan" element of the ISO27001 process also addresses the third element of the legal process. It requires companies to "select control objectives and controls for the treatment of risks"[48] (*see Section 5.3*). Like applicable law, ISO27001 requires that "control objectives and controls shall be selected and implemented to meet the requirements identified by the risk assessment and the risk treatment process." It also requires that this selection "take account of the criteria for accepting risks[49] as well as legal, regulatory and contractual requirements."

For purposes of selecting appropriate security controls, ISO27001 refers to a list of control objectives and controls that are directly derived from and aligned with those listed in ISO27002. Those controls essentially include all of the controls listed in Chapter 6. However, it also notes that the listed control objectives and controls are not exhaustive and

---

[47] ISO27001, §§ 4.2.1(c), (d), (e), and (f).
[48] ISO27001, § 4.2.1(g).
[49] ISO27001, § 4.2.1(c)(2).

additional control objectives and controls may also be selected.

Do (implement and operate the ISMS): The "do" element of the ISO27001 process essentially corresponds to the part of the legal process described above relating to the implementation of security controls to manage and control the risks identified (*see Section 5.3*). The key requirements of the "do" element of the ISO27001 process are to implement the controls selected,[50] define how to measure the effectiveness of the selected controls,[51] and implement training and awareness programs.[52]

Check (monitor and review the ISMS): The "check" element of the ISO27001 process corresponds to the fourth element of the legal process identified above – i.e. monitor and test the program to ensure that it is effective (*see Section 5.4*). Specifically, the "check" element of the ISO27001 process requires that companies "execute monitoring and reviewing procedures" to promptly detect errors, identify attempted and successful security breaches, and determine whether actions taken to resolve a breach were effective. It also requires regular reviews of the effectiveness of the ISMS and measurements of the effectiveness of the controls to verify that security requirements have been met.

The "check" element of the ISO27001 process also corresponds to the fifth element of the legal process in that it requires continual review and adjustment of the program in light of on going changes (*see Section 5.5*) Specifically,

---

[50] ISO27001, § 4.2.2(c).
[51] ISO27001, § 4.2.2(d).
[52] ISO27001, § 4.2.2(e).

it requires that companies review risk assessments at planned intervals and review the residual risks and the identified acceptable levels of risk, taking into account changes to "(1) the organization; (2) technology; (3) business objectives and processes; (4) identified threats; (5) effectiveness of the implemented controls; and (6) external events, such as changes to the legal or regulatory environment, changed contractual obligations, and changes in social climate."[53] It also requires companies to conduct regular internal ISMS audits "to determine whether the control objectives, controls, processes and procedures of its ISMS" conform to the requirements of ISO27001 and relevant legislation or regulations, conform to the identified security requirements, are effectively implemented and maintained, and perform as expected.[54]

Act (maintain and improve the ISMS): The final part of the PDCA process is basically a recognition that the security process is an ongoing activity that is never finished. Accordingly, it requires the company to implement identified improvements in the ISMS, to take appropriate corrective and preventive actions to apply lessons learned from the security experiences of other organizations as well as its own, and to insure that the improvements achieve their intended objectives.[55]

Documentation requirements: Like the legal standard, ISO27001 requires that the security program (the ISMS) be appropriately and adequately documented in writing. In particular, it notes that: "it is important to be able to demonstrate the relationship from the selected controls back

---

[53] ISO27001, § 4.2.3(d).
[54] ISO27001, § 6. See also § 4.2.3(e).
[55] ISO27001, § 4.2.4.

to the results of the risk assessment and risk treatment process, and subsequently back to the ISMS policy and objectives."[56] In addition, it requires that the company establish and maintain records "to provide evidence of conformity to requirements in the effective operation of the ISMS."[57]

Management responsibility: ISO27001 also makes clear that management has overall responsibility for the development and implementation of the company's information security program. It requires that "management shall provide evidence of its commitment to the establishment, implementation, operation, monitoring, review, maintenance and improvement of the ISMS."[58] In addition to establishing the ISMS, this includes communicating its importance to the company, providing sufficient resources to create and implement it, and reviewing it at regular intervals "to insure its continuing suitability, adequacy and effectiveness."[59]

---

[56] ISO27001, § 4.3.1.
[57] ISO27001, § 4.3.3.
[58] ISO27001, § 5.1.
[59] ISO27001, § 7.1

CHAPTER 8: SECURITY BREACH NOTIFICATION

In addition to the legal obligation to *implement* security measures to protect corporate data, many laws enacted during the past few years impose an obligation to *disclose* security breaches to the persons affected. But unlike laws that impose a duty to provide security, these laws typically require only that companies disclose security breaches to those who may be adversely affected by such breaches.[1]

For the most part, laws imposing an obligation to disclose security breaches began as a direct reaction to a series of well-publicized security breaches involving sensitive personal information over the past few years,[2] and as part of an effort to address the problem of identity theft. A total of 44 states in the US, plus the District of Columbia, Puerto Rico, and the Virgin Islands, have enacted security breach notification laws as of September 2008, all generally based on a 2003 California law.[3] The US federal banking regulatory agencies also require financial institutions to disclose breaches.[4] And as discussed below, the concept of breach notification is rapidly becoming recognized internationally.

---

[1] *Pisciotta v. Old National Bancorp.* 2007 US App. Lexis 20068 (7th Cir. 23 August 2007), p. 13.

[2] For a chronology of such breaches in the US and a running total of the number of individuals affected, see Privacy Rights Clearinghouse at www.privacyrights.org/ar/ChronDataBreaches.htm.

[3] See list of statutes in Appendix.

[4] Interagency Guidance on Response Programs for Unauthorized Access to Customer Information and Customer Notice, Part III of Supplement A to Appendix, at 12 CFR Part 30 (OCC), 12 CFR Part 208 (Federal Reserve System), 12 CFR Part 364 (FDIC), and 12 CFR Part 568 (Office of Thrift Supervision), March 29, 2005, Federal Register, Vol. 70, No. 59, 29 March 2005, p. 15736 (hereinafter "Interagency Guidance").

These breach notification statutes raise numerous novel and undecided issues. Moreover, no legislative history is available for guidance and, to date, none of these statutes have been the subject of any significant interpretation by any court or regulator.[5]

8.1 Objectives of the breach notification laws

The breach notification statutes are intended to help protect persons who might be adversely affected by a compromise of certain categories of sensitive personally identifiable information (PII). To do that, these statutes impose on companies that maintain such PII an obligation to notify persons who may be at risk by a breach of the security of that information (e.g. persons whose compromised PII may be used to facilitate identity theft or unauthorized access to bank accounts, credit cards, etc.).

In effect, these laws impose on companies an obligation similar to the common law "duty to warn" of dangers. Such a duty is often based on the view that a party who has a superior knowledge of a danger of injury or damage to another that is posed by a specific hazard must warn those who lack such knowledge. By requiring notice to persons

---

[5] The only cases as of July 2008 are: *Ponder v. Pfizer, Inc.* 2007 US Dist. Lexis 83129 (M.D. La. Nov. 7, 2007) (noting that the Louisiana breach law provides for a private right of action); *Pisciotta v. Old Nat'l Bancorp*, 499 F.3d 629 (7th Cir. 2007) (noting that the Indiana breach law requires only that a database owner disclose a security breach to potentially affected consumers, that it does not require the database owner to take any other affirmative act in the wake of a breach, and that if the database owner fails to comply with the duty to disclose, the statute provides for enforcement *only* by the Attorney General of Indiana – i.e. it creates no private right of action against the database owner by an affected customer and imposes no duty to compensate affected individuals for inconvenience or potential harm to credit that may follow); and *Parke v. CardSystems Solutions, Inc.* 2006 US Dist. Lexis 77241 (N.D. Cal. 11 October 2006) (noting that there appears to be no reported appellate decisions interpreting the California breach law).

who may be adversely affected by a security breach (e.g. persons whose compromised personal information may be used to facilitate identity theft), these laws seek to provide such persons with a warning that their personal information has been compromised, and an opportunity to take steps to protect themselves against the consequences of identity theft.[6]

Breach notification laws and regulations do not, by themselves, directly require a company to *implement* any security measures.[7] Instead, they impose an obligation to *disclose* security breaches when they occur. But they may have a significant impact on corporate security obligations.

Specifically, breach notification laws leverage a very powerful force – the fact that the required disclosures may be embarrassing and serve to publicly highlight a company's lack of adequate security. Absent a legal requirement, most companies do not publicly disclose information security breaches or contact law enforcement agencies. The annual Computer Security Institute and FBI Computer Crime and Security Survey for 2005,[8] for example, reported that only 20 percent of respondents who suffered serious computer security breaches reported the incident to law enforcement. The key reason cited for not reporting intrusions to law enforcement, according to the report, is the concern for negative publicity. Thus, the fear of adverse publicity arising from the obligation to disclose

---

[6] See e.g. Office of Privacy Protection, California Department of Consumer Affairs, *Recommended Practices on Notification of Security Breach Involving Personal Information*, February, 2007, pp. 5-6 (available at www.oispp.ca.gov/consumer_privacy/pdf/secbreach.pdf).
[7] Although some states have enacted such an obligation. See list of US state laws imposing obligations to provide security for personal information in Appendix.
[8] Available at www.gocsi.com.

security breaches may actually incentivize companies to implement better security measures in the first place, so as to minimize breaches that might require public disclosure. Federal banking regulations directly address this issue, and expressly state: "when customer notification is warranted, an institution may not forgo notifying its customers of an incident because the institution believes that it may be potentially embarrassed or inconvenienced by doing so."[9]

8.2 Viewing the laws in perspective

Although the vast majority of security breach notification laws have been enacted in the past few years, such laws are not new. Moreover, their scope is not necessarily limited to security breaches involving customers' personal information, or even personal information generally.

In fact, as far back as 1994 the Minnesota Computer Crime Statute imposed a reporting requirement of sorts. That statute prohibits the unauthorized access, alteration, damage, or destruction of any computer, network, or software, as well as penetration of a computer security system and the distribution of a destructive computer program (e.g. a virus or worm).[10] And it includes a requirement that a person "who has reason to believe" that any provision of the statute is being or has been violated "shall report the suspected violation to the prosecuting authority in the county in which all or a part of the suspected violation occurred."[11] Since this requirement applies to any person with knowledge, it clearly includes a

---

[9] See Interagency Guidance, p. 15752.
[10] See Minn. Stat. §§ 609.88, 609.89, and 609.891.
[11] Minn. Stat. Section 609.891.

business that suffers a breach of security, at least where the breach also constitutes a violation of the statute.

In 1998 the US Internal Revenue Service (IRS) also imposed a disclosure requirement on all taxpayers whose electronic tax records were the subject of a security breach. In a regulation that sets forth its basic rules for maintaining tax-related records in electronic form, the IRS requires taxpayers to "promptly notify" the IRS District Director if any electronic tax records "are lost, stolen, destroyed, damaged, or otherwise no longer capable of being processed ..., or are found to be incomplete or materially inaccurate."[12] The notice must identify the affected records and include a plan that describes how, and in what time frame, the taxpayer proposes to replace or restore the affected records in a way that assures that they will be capable of being processed.[13]

With respect to breaches involving personal information, the first, and most widely publicized, law requiring disclosure of security breaches was the California Security Breach Information Act (S.B. 1386), which became effective on July 1, 2003.[14] That law requires all companies doing business in California to disclose any breach of security that results in an unauthorized person acquiring certain types of personally identifiable information of a California resident. Disclosure must be made to all persons whose personal information was compromised, and anyone who is injured by a company's failure to do so can sue to recover damages. It is this law

---

[12] IRS Rev. Proc. 98-25, § 8.01.
[13] IRS Rev. Proc. 98-25, § 8.02.
[14] Cal. Civil Code Section 1798.82. A copy is available at www.leginfo.ca.gov/calaw.html.

that has served as the model for all of the additional state laws enacted starting in 2005.

Some other countries also have laws that either expressly or impliedly impose similar disclosure requirements.[15] And in September, 2006, the European Commission proposed that all providers of "electronic communications networks or services" be required to notify consumers and regulators about security breaches.[16]

8.3 The breach notification obligation

Taken as a group, the breach notification laws generally require that any business in possession of computerized sensitive personal information about an individual must disclose a breach of the security of such information to the person affected.[17] What constitutes sensitive personal information, when a triggering event occurs, and the notice requirements themselves, are the subject of much debate. In general, however, the key requirements, which vary from statute to statute, include the following:

---

[15] See Ethan Preston and Paul Turner, *The Global Rise of a Duty to Disclose Information Security Breaches*, 22 J. Marshall Computer & Info. L. 457 (Winter 2004).

[16] See Communication from the Commission to the Council, the European Parliament, The European Economic and Social Committee and the Committee of the Regions on the Review of the EU Regulatory Framework for electronic communications networks and services {COM(2006) 334 final}, June 28, 2006, Section 7.2, available at http://europa.eu.int/information_society/policy/ecomm/doc/info_centre/public_consult/re view/staffworkingdocument_final.pdf.

[17] Except where the business maintains computerized personal information that the business does not own, in which case the laws require the business to notify the owner or licensee of the information, rather than the individuals themselves, of any breach of the security of the system.

8.3.1 Covered information

Security breach notification laws generally apply to all "sensitive personal information" in a company's possession or control. These laws generally require that any business in possession of computerized sensitive personal information about an individual must disclose a breach of the security of such information to the person affected.

The statutes typically define sensitive personal information as information consisting of (1) a person's first name or initial and last name, plus (2) any one of the following: Social Security number, driver's license or state ID number, or financial account number or credit or debit card number. In some states this list is longer, and may also include medical information, insurance policy numbers, passwords, biometric information, professional license or permit numbers, telecommunication access codes, mother's maiden name, employer ID number, electronic signatures, and descriptions of an individual's personal characteristics.[18]

8.3.2 Triggering event

Generally, the event that triggers the obligation to provide notice is any unauthorized acquisition of unencrypted computerized data that compromises the security, confidentiality or integrity of an individual's sensitive personal information. In other words, almost any breach of security relating to unencrypted sensitive personal information will trigger notice obligations in most states.

---

[18] See e.g. Arkansas, Delaware, New York, North Carolina, and North Dakota statutes.

Under some statutes, however, even if a breach occurs, notice is not required in cases where there is no reasonable likelihood of harm (or some variation thereof) to the persons whose information is compromised. There are a number of approaches to this "likelihood of harm" exception in the breach notification statutes which can be summarized as follows:

- *Focus on likelihood of loss or injury.* Notification is not required where the security breach is: not reasonably likely to cause substantial economic loss (Arizona); not likely to cause substantial loss or injury to, or result in identity theft (Michigan); not reasonably believed to cause loss or injury (Montana and Pennsylvania); and creates no reasonable likelihood of harm (Arkansas, Connecticut, Florida, Louisiana and Oregon).
- *Focus on likelihood of misuse of the information.* Notification is not required where: misuse of information not reasonably likely to occur (Colorado, Delaware, Idaho, Kansas, Maryland, New Hampshire, Utah and Wyoming), misuse of the information is not reasonably possible (New Jersey, Vermont and Maine), use of information for an unauthorized purpose is not reasonably likely to occur (Massachusetts and Nebraska), and illegal use of the personal information is not reasonably likely to occur and presents no material risk of harm (North Carolina and Hawaii).
- *Focus on identity theft.* Notification is not required where (or unless) the security breach: could result in identity deception . . . identity theft, or fraud (Indiana), will not likely result in a significant risk of identity theft (Rhode Island), will not cause a material risk of identity theft or other fraud (Ohio and Wisconsin), and does not

create a substantial risk of identity theft or fraud, or use for unauthorized purpose (Massachusetts).

8.3.3 *Who must be notified*

Under each statute, notice must be given to the residents of the enacting jurisdiction whose unencrypted personal information was the subject of the breach. The problem, of course, is that it's not always possible to determine whose information was compromised. In such a case, an over-inclusive notification may be required.

In addition to notifying the individuals affected by the breach, in certain cases some statutes also require that notice be given to government enforcement agencies, such as the state Attorney General's office or the police, as well as to consumer reporting agencies.[19] This typically occurs where more than a specified number of individuals are involved (e.g. more than 1,000).

8.3.4 *What must be included in the notice*

Most security breach notification statutes do not specify the contents of the notice. However, in those that do, the general view is the notice should be "clear and conspicuous" and should include the following information:[20]

- a description of the incident in general terms;

---

[19] States with such provisions include Florida, Minnesota, Nevada, New Jersey, New York, North Carolina, and Tennessee.
[20] See e.g. N.C. Gen. Stat. § 75-65(d); N.Y. Act § 6; California Recommended Practices, p. 12; and Interagency Guidance, p. 15736.

- a description of the type of personal information that was the subject of unauthorized access or use;

- a description of what the company has done to protect the individuals' information from further unauthorized access;

- a description of what the company will do to assist individuals, including a telephone number or other contact information so that recipients of the notice can call for further information and assistance;

- information on what individuals can do to protect themselves from identity theft, including contact information for the three credit reporting agencies and

- contact information for agencies (e.g. the FTC) that can provide additional information on protection against identity theft.

8.3.5 Timing of the notice

Generally, most of the statutes require that persons whose information is compromised via a security breach must be notified "in the most expedient time possible and without unreasonable delay."[21] Some state statutes also establish a maximum time period.[22] The federal Interagency Guidance, on the other hand, simply indicates that after a determination that misuse has occurred or is reasonably possible, the affected customer should be notified "as soon as possible."[23]

---

[21] See e.g. California Civil Code § 1798.92(a). Similar language appears in most statutes.
[22] Connecticut, § 4(a) (not later than 15 days after discovery of the breach); Florida, § 817.5681(1)(a) (without unreasonably delay, but not later than 45 days).
[23] See Interagency Guidance, at p. 15752.

Most breach notification laws authorize delay in certain cases. In most states delivery of the notice may be delayed for the following reasons:

- legitimate needs of law enforcement, if notification would impede a criminal investigation; or
- taking necessary measures to determine the scope of the breach and restore reasonable integrity to the system.

It is important to note, however, that in some cases the right to delay notice for law enforcement purposes is available only if an appropriate law enforcement agency determines that notification will interfere with a criminal investigation and provides the company with a written request for the delay.[24]   Moreover, the company should notify its customers as soon as notification will no longer interfere with the investigation.

8.3.6 Form of notice

Almost all laws specify that notice may be provided in one of the following forms:

- in writing (e.g. on paper and sent by mail);
- in electronic form (e.g. by e-mail, but only if the individual has consented in advance to receive the notice in electronic form in accordance with the procedures of the federal E-SIGN law); or
- by substitute notice.

As an alternative, most state statutes also authorize businesses to use their own notification procedures if such

---

[24] Id.

procedures have been previously adopted as part of the company's information security policy for personal information. In such case, however, the company's notification procedures must be consistent with the timing requirements of the statute and the company must notify the affected individuals in accordance with its policy.[25] This clearly provides an incentive to develop an incident response plan.

The federal Interagency Guidance takes a slightly different approach, as it focuses on likelihood of receipt rather than specific form of notice. Specifically, it provides that:

> Customer notice should be delivered *in any manner* designed to ensure that a customer can reasonably be expected to receive it. For example, the institution may choose to contact all customers affected by telephone or by mail, or by electronic mail for those customers for whom it has a valid e-mail address and who have agreed to receive communications electronically.[26]

E-mail notice requirements: In most cases, the general right to provide notice by e-mail is somewhat illusory. It is available, of course, only if the company actually has current e-mail addresses for the affected individuals. But more importantly, the e-mail option is usually available only if the notice is provided consistent with the requirements of the federal E-SIGN Act.[27]

Under E-SIGN, sending a breach notification notice to a consumer in electronic form is acceptable only if the consumer affirmatively consents to receive an electronic

---

[25] See e.g. California Civil Code § 1798.92(h). Similar language appears in most statutes.

[26] See e.g. Interagency Guidance, p. 15753 (emphasis added).

[27] Electronic Signatures in Global and National Commerce Act (hereinafter "E-SIGN"), 15 USC 7001 *et. seq.*

notice in lieu of a paper notice, provides such consent electronically, and does so in a manner that "reasonably demonstrates" that he or she can access the electronic information in the form that will be used.[28] Moreover, prior to consenting, the consumer must be provided with a clear and conspicuous notice that informs the consumer of:

- his/her option to have the information provided on paper;
- the procedures the consumer must use to update information needed to contact the consumer electronically;
- after consent, how he/she may obtain a paper copy of the electronic notice, and the fee therefore;
- the hardware and software requirements for access and retention of the electronic notice;
- his/her option to withdraw such consent, and the procedures the consumer must use to withdraw consent; and
- the conditions, consequences, and fees of withdrawing such consent.[29]

Failure to comply with the requirements of E-SIGN would presumably render the e-mail notice ineffective.

Substitute notice options: The option of substitute notice is available in all states that have passed security breach notification laws. It is not, however, specifically mentioned in the federal Interagency Guidance.

---

[28] E-SIGN, 15 USC §§ 7001(c)(1)(A) and 7001(c)(1)(C)(ii).
[29] E-SIGN, 15 USC § 7001(c)(1).

Generally, if the cost of providing individual notice is greater than a certain amount ($250,000 in most states) or if more than a certain number of people would have to be notified (500,000 in most states), substitute notice may be used. Substitute notice typically consists of all of the following:

- sending the notice by e-mail to those individuals for whom an e-mail address is available (presumably without E-SIGN compliance); and
- conspicuously posting the notice on the company's web site; and
- notification in all major statewide media (television, radio, and print).

8.3.7 Penalties

Most laws provide some mechanism for state enforcement of the security breach notification laws, usually by the state's Attorney General or a similar state official. Several state statutes also expressly provide for a private right of action, whereby persons injured by a failure to comply with the statute can sue the company for damages.

8.4 International adoption

Although the breach notification concept began in the US, it is rapidly spreading to the international sector.[30] Japan became the first country outside the US to impose a security breach notification obligation. The obligation is

---

[30] See Ethan Preston and Paul Turner, *The Global Rise of a Duty to Disclose Information Security Breaches*, 22 J. Marshall Computer & Info. L. 457 (Winter 2004).

set forth in ministry guidelines to the Act on the Protection of Personal Information, which took effect for the private sector on April 1, 2005.[31]

In September, 2006, the European Commission (EC) released a communication proposing changes to EU law that would require "electronic communications networks or services" to "notify their customers of any breach of security leading to the loss, modification or destruction of, or unauthorized access to, personal customer data." As the Commission pointed out: "A requirement to notify security breaches would create an incentive for providers to invest in security but without micro-managing their security policies."[32]

Later in the same month, the data protection authorities responsible for steering the implementation of the EU Data Protection Directive (known as the Article 29 Working Party) released an opinion in which it sought to expand the scope of data breach notification. Specifically, the document expressed concerns about the lack of sanctions for telecommunication operators and ISPs if they do not inform customers about data breaches, and included a recommendation that the breach notification obligation should also cover data brokers, banks and other online service providers.[33]

---

[31] See Miriam Wugmeister, Saori Horikawa, and Daniel Levison, *What You Need to Know About Japan's New Law Concerning the Protection of Personal Information*, BNA Privacy & Security Law Report, Volume 4 Number 19, p. 614, 9 May 2005.

[32] See Communication on the Review of the EU Regulatory Framework for electronic communications networks and services {COM (2006) 334 final} 28 June 2006, at http://europa.eu.int/information_society/policy/ecomm/doc/info_centre/public_consult/re view/staffworkingdocument_final.pdf.

[33] Article 29 Data Protection Working Party, "Opinion 8/2006 on the review of the regulatory Framework for Electronic Communications and Services, with focus on the

In the UK, a July 2007 report by the Select Committee on Science and Technology on the Internet and Personal Safety of the House of Lords also recommended adoption of security breach notification legislation. Specifically, it stated that:

We further believe that a data security breach notification law would be among the most important advances that the United Kingdom could make in promoting personal Internet security. We recommend that the Government, without waiting for action at European Commission level, accept the principle of such a law, and begin consultation on its scope as a matter of urgency.[34]

In Canada, the Office of the Privacy Commissioner issued voluntary guidelines for responding to data breaches in August 2007. Pointing out that "notification can be an important mitigation strategy" that benefits both the organization and the individuals affected by a breach, the guidelines indicated that "if a privacy breach creates a risk of harm to the individual, those affected should be notified" in order to help them mitigate the damage by taking steps to protect themselves.[35]

Shortly thereafter, the Privacy Commissioner in New Zealand released similar guidelines.[36] Although the New Zealand guidelines are voluntary, the Privacy Commissioner noted that "principle 5 of the Privacy Act (governing the way personal information is stored) does

ePrivacy Directive," adopted on 26 September 2006, available at http://ec.europa.eu/justice_home/fsj/privacy/docs/wpdocs/2006/wp126_en.pdf.

[34] Science and Technology Committee, House of Lords, *Personal Internet Security, 5th Report of Session 2006–07*, 24 July 2007, Para. 5.55.

[35] Office of the Privacy Commissioner of Canada, *Key Steps for Organizations in Responding to Privacy Breaches*, 28 August 2007; available at www.privcom.gc.ca/information/guide/2007/gl_070801_02_e.asp.

[36] See Privacy Breach Guidance Material, Office of the Privacy Commissioner, August 2007, available at www.privacy.org.nz/library/privacy-breach-guidelines.

require all organizations and individuals that hold personal information to take reasonable steps to protect it. This can include notifying people of significant breaches, where necessary."[37]

The Australian Privacy Commissioner also recommended that Australia consider amending its privacy legislation to include a mandatory requirement to report security breaches involving personal information. Her February 28, 2007 submission to the Australian Law Reform Commission supported "consideration of the addition of provisions to the Privacy Act to require agencies and organizations to advise affected individuals of a breach to their personal information in certain circumstances."[38] On August 18, 2008, the Australian Law Reform Commission released its report titled *For Your Information: Australian Privacy Law and Practice*[39] which proposed numerous changes to Australia's privacy law. Included among the proposals was a new system of data breach notification.[40]

8.5 What companies need to do

Most companies doing business in several jurisdictions are likely subject to different breach notification laws. Thus, as a practical matter, organizations will probably be required to apply the strictest standard to all of their notification

---

[37] Privacy Commissioner, Media Release, 27 August 2007, available at www.privacy.org.nz/privacy-breach-guidelines-2/.
[38] See Australian Government, Office of the Privacy Commissioner, Submission to the Australian Law Reform Commission's Review of Privacy - Issues Paper 31, 28 February 2007, paragraphs 127-129; available at www.privacy.gov.au/publications/submissions/alrc/all.pdf.
[39] Available at www.austlii.edu.au/au/other/alrc/publications/reports/108/.
[40] Id. at Section 51.

practices. For while it is certainly possible that a specific security breach will trigger notice obligations under some breach notification laws, but not under others, the public relations risk of giving notice to some, but not to others may be unacceptable.

This argues for careful planning. How a company prepares for and responds to security breaches when they occur is a key issue. Prompt action on a variety of fronts is critical, both from a legal and a public relations perspective.

8.5.1 *Information review*

Given the proliferation of security breach notification laws, and the resulting duty to disclose breaches, there is a premium on taking steps, in advance, to reduce or eliminate the risk of having to make a disclosure. Perhaps the most basic step in this area is to reduce or eliminate the amount of notice-triggering information that the company collects and maintains.

This begins with a review of information collection practices, both to identify where sensitive personal information is collected and stored, and to assess whether such information is really needed. In many cases, information subject to the security breach notification laws may not even be needed. But if it is, the company must have an accurate understanding and inventory of what sensitive personal data it collects, how it is used, and where it is stored. The bottom line is to identify and properly manage notice-triggering information, and if not needed, eliminate its collection and storage.

8.5.2 Implement security measures

The next step, of course, is to ensure that appropriate security measures are in place to protect the sensitive personal information the company does collect, use, and store. To the extent that appropriate security can prevent breaches, and thus avoid the need for disclosure, it will be well worth the effort. Moreover, as discussed in the preceding chapters, such security is likely a legal obligation in any event. Thus, organizations should ensure that they have effectively addressed compliance with their duty to provide security.

Also worth noting is the fact that most security breach notification statutes apply only to the compromise of unencrypted personal information. Thus, to the extent reasonably feasible, encryption of all relevant personal information may well help to avoid the need to make embarrassing disclosures.

8.5.3 Incident response planning

Regardless of the level of security implemented, breaches may still be inevitable. Thus, it is also important to recognize that, as part of a comprehensive security program, companies need to develop and implement a well thought out and legally compliant incident response plan. In other words, how will the company respond if a breach does occur?

An incident response plan should ensure that appropriate persons within the organization are promptly notified of security breaches, and that prompt action is taken both in terms of responding to the breach (e.g. to stop further information compromise and to work with law enforcement), and in terms of notifying appropriate persons who may be potentially injured by the breach.

Such a plan should also clearly address how the company will comply with the differing requirements of the applicable security breach notification laws. This includes addressing issues such as whether a triggering event has occurred, how the affected individuals will be identified, the content, form and style of the notices, how notices will be communicated to the affected individuals, coordination with law enforcement (where relevant), and coordination with consumer reporting agencies.

It is also worth noting that development of an incident response plan can give companies flexibility in the procedures that can be used to notify persons affected by a breach. Specifically, most states allow companies to develop their own alternate to the statutory notification requirements. So long as the business "maintains its own notification procedures as part of an information security policy for the treatment of personal information," and as long as those notification procedures are "consistent with the timing requirements" of the state's breach notification statute, the company will be deemed to be in compliance with the notification requirements of the statute if, in the event of a security breach, it notifies affected persons in accordance with its notification procedures.

8.5.4 *Third party issues*

Finally, all planning needs to consider sensitive personal information in the control of third parties, such as business partners and third party service providers. Outsourcing information processing to a third party does not relieve a company of its obligations with respect to the security of the information outsourced, or its obligations to make disclosures in the event such information is the subject of a security breach. As a consequence, businesses will need to look carefully at the security measures of the outsource providers with whom they contract, and the measures in place (contractual and otherwise) to respond to breaches. Business partners and third party service providers should also be required to participate in and comply with requirements of the organization's incident response plan where appropriate.

* * *

Taken as a group, these new security breach notification laws suggest a key new addition to the law on corporate information security obligations – one that goes well beyond the duty of a company to provide security for its information – by adding a duty to warn those who might be adversely impacted by a failure of, or lack of, corporate security. Implicit in such an approach is recognition of the wide-ranging impact of a company's electronic activities, and the fact that security vulnerabilities in a company can have a significant adverse impact on a wide variety of stakeholders.

APPENDIX

*Statutes, regulations, and cases
imposing information security obligations*

A. US federal statutes

1. **COPPA**: Children's Online Privacy Protection Act of 1998, 15 USC 6501 *et seq.*

2. **E-SIGN**: Electronic Signatures in Global and National Commerce Act, 15 USC § 7001(d).

3. **FCRA/FACTA:** Fair Credit Reporting Act.

4. **FISMA**: Federal Information Security Management Act of 2002, 44 USC Sections 3541-3549.

5. **FTC Act:** Federal Trade Commission Act, 15 USC § 45(a)(1), prohibits unfair or deceptive acts or practices in or affecting commerce.

6. **GLB Act**: Gramm-Leach-Bliley Financial Services Modernization Act, Public L. 106-102, Sections 501 and 505(b), 15 USC Sections 6801, 6805.

7. **HIPAA**: Health Insurance Portability and Accountability Act of 1996, 42 USC 1320d-2 and 1320d-4.

8. **Homeland Security Act of 2002**: 44 USC Section 3532(b)(1).

9. **Privacy Act of 1974:** 5 USC Section 552a.

10. **Sarbanes-Oxley Act of 2002**: Pub. L. 107-204, 116 Stat. 745, Sections 302 and 404, 15 USC Sections

7241 and 7262, also known as the Public Company Accounting Reform and Investor Protection Act, and commonly called SOX or Sarbox.

11. **Federal Rules of Evidence 901(a):** see *American Express v. Vinhnee*, 2005 Bankr. LEXIS 2602 (9th Cir. Bk. App. Panel, 2005), and *Lorraine v. Markel*, 2007 US Dist. LEXIS 33020 (D. Md. May 4, 2007).

B. US state statutes

1. **UETA:** Uniform Electronic Transaction Act, Section 12 (now enacted in 46 states).

2. **Laws imposing obligation to provide security for personal information:**

   Arkansas: Ark. Code Ann. § 4-110-104(b)
   California: Cal. Civ. Code § 1798.81.5(b)
   Connecticut: Public Act No. 08-167
   Maryland: Md. Commercial Law Code Ann. § 14-3503
   Massachusetts: Mass. Gen. Laws. Ch. 93H, § 2(a)
   Nevada: Nev. Rev. Stat. 603A.210
   Rhode Island: R.I. Stat. 11-49.2-2(2) and (3)
   Oregon: 2007 S.B. 583, Section 12
   Texas: Tex. Bus. & Com. Code Ann. § 48.102(a)
   Utah: Utah Code Ann. § 13-44-20.

3. **Laws imposing obligation to provide security for credit card information:**

   Minnesota: Minn. Stat. Chapter 325E.64.

4. **Data disposal / destruction laws:**

   Alaska: Ala. Stat. §§ 45.48.500 – 45.48.590
   Arkansas: Ark. Code Ann. § 4-110-104(a)

California: Cal. Civil Code § 1798.81.
Connecticut: Public Act No. 08-167
Georgia: Ga. Stat. § 10-15-2
Hawaii: Haw. Stat. Section § 487R-2
Illinois: 815 ILCS 530/30 (state agencies only)
Indiana: Ind. Code § 24-4-14
Kentucky: Ken. Rev. Stat. § 365.720
Maryland: Md. Code § 14-3502
Massachusetts: Mass. Gen. Laws. Ch. 93I
Michigan: MCL § 445.72a
Montana: Mont. Stat. § 30-14-1703
Nevada: Nev. Rev. Stat. 603A.200
New Jersey: N.J. Stat. 56:8-162
North Carolina: N.C. Gen. Stat. § 75-64
Oregon: 2007 S.B. 583, Section 12
Texas: Tex. Bus. & Com. Code Ann. § 48.102(b)
Utah: Utah Code Ann. § 13-42-201
Vermont: Vt. Stat. Tit. 9 § 2445 *et seq.*
Washington: RCWA 19.215.020.

5. **Security breach notification laws**

Alaska: Ala. Stat. §§ 45.48.010 – 45.48.090
Arizona: Ariz. Rev. Stat. § 44-7501
Arkansas: Ark. Code § 4-110-101 *et seq.*
California: Cal. Civ. Code § 1798.82
Colorado: Col. Rev. Stat. § 6-1-716
Connecticut: Conn. Gen. Stat. 36A-701(b)
Delaware: De. Code Tit. 6, § 12B-101 *et seq.*
Dist. of Columbia: DC Code § 28-3851 *et seq.*
Florida: Fla. Stat. § 817.5681
Georgia: Ga. Code § 10-1-910 *et seq.*
Hawaii: Hawaii Rev. Stat. § 487N-2

Appendix

Idaho: Id. Code §§ 28-51-104 to 28-51-107
Illinois: 815 Ill. Comp. Stat. 530/1 *et seq.*
Indiana: Ind. Code § 24-4.9
Iowa: 2008 Iowa S.F. 2308
Kansas: Kansas Stat. 50-7a01, 50-7a02
Louisiana: La. Rev. Stat. § 51:3071 *et seq.*
Maine: Me. Rev. Stat. Tit. 10 §§ 1347 *et seq.*
Maryland: Md. Code, §§ 14-3501 thru 14-3508
Massachusetts: Mass. Gen. Laws. Ch. 93H
Michigan: MCL 445.63, Sections 12, 12a, & 12b
Minnesota: Minn. Stat. § 325E.61, § 609.891
Montana: Mont. Code § 30-14-1701 *et seq.*
Nebraska: Neb. Rev. Stat 87-801 *et seq.*
Nevada: Nev. Rev. Stat. 603A.010 *et seq.*
New Hampshire: N.H. RS 359-C:19 *et seq.*
New Jersey: N.J. Stat. 56:8-163
New York: N.Y. Bus. Law § 899-aa
North Carolina: N.C. Gen. Stat. § 75-65
North Dakota: N.D. Cent. Code § 51-30-01 *et seq.*
Ohio: Ohio Rev. Code § 1349.19, §1347 *et seq.*
Oklahoma: Okla. Stat. Tit. 24, § 161, *et seq.*
Oregon: Oregon: ORS § 646A
Pennsylvania: 73 Pa. Cons. Stat. § 2303
Puerto Rico: 2005 H.B. 1184
Rhode Island: R.I. Gen. Laws § 11-49.2-1 *et seq.*
South Carolina: S.C. Code § 39-1-90
Tennessee: Tenn. Code § 47-18-2107
Texas: Tex. Bus. & Com. Code § 48.001 *et seq.*
Utah: Utah Code § 13-44-101 *et seq.*
Vermont: Vt. Stat. Tit. 9 § 2430 *et seq.*
Virgin Islands (US): 4 V.I.C. § 2209 (2007)
Virginia: Va. Code 18.2-186.6
Washington: Wash. Rev. Code § 19.255.010

West Virginia: W. Va. Code §§46A-2A-101 – 46A-2A-105

Wisconsin: Wis. Stat. § 895.507

Wyoming: Wyo. Stat. §§ 40-12-501 – 40-12-502.

6. Social Security number laws

Alaska: Ala. Stat. §§ 45.48.400 – 45.48.480

Arizona: Ariz. Rev. Stat. § 44-1373

Arkansas: Ark. Code Ann. § 4-86-107; § 6-18-208

California: Cal. Civ. Code § 1798.85; Fam. Code § 2024.5

Colorado: Colo. Rev. Stat. § 6-1-715; § 23-5-127;

Connecticut: Conn. Gen. Stat. § 8-64b; § 42-470; and Public Act 08-167

Delaware: Del. Code Ann. Tit. 7 § 503

Florida: Fla. Stat. Ch. 97.05851

Georgia: Ga. Code Ann. § 10-1-393.8; § 50-18-72

Hawaii: Haw. Rev. Stat. § 12-32; §§ 487J-2 to 487J-3

Illinois: 815 Ill. Comp. Stat. 505/2QQ3 and 505/2RR

Indiana: Ind. Code § 4-1-10-1 *et seq.*; § 9-24-6-2; § 9-24-9-2; § 9-24-11-5; § 9-24-16-3; §§ 24-4-14-1 to 24-4-14-8

Kansas: Kan. Stat. Ann. § 75-3520

Louisiana: La. Rev. Stat. Ann. 9:5141; 35:17

Maine: Me. Rev. Stat. Ann. Tit. 10 § 1272-B

Maryland: Md. Code Ann. Com. Law § 14-3401 *et seq.*

Massachusetts: Mass. Gen. Laws Ch. 167B, § 14 & § 22

Michigan: Mich. Comp. Laws § 445.81 *et seq.*

Minnesota: Minn. Stat. § 325E.59

Missouri: Mo. Rev. Stat. § 407.1355

Montana: Mont. Code Ann. § 30-14-1702, § 30-14-1703

Nebraska: Neb. Rev. Stat. § 48-237

Nevada: Nev. Rev. Stat. Chapter 239; Chapter 239B; Chapter 603

New Jersey: N.J. Stat. Ann. § 47:1-16

New Mexico: N.M. Stat. Ann. § 57-12B-1 *et seq.*

New York: N.Y. Gen. Bus. Law § 399-dd

North Carolina: N.C. Gen. Stat. §§ 75-62

North Dakota: N.D. Cent. Code § 39-06-14

Oklahoma: Okla. Stat. Tit. 40, § 173.1

Oregon: Ore. Als. 759

Pennsylvania: 74 Pa. Stat. Ann. §§ 201 to 204

Rhode Island: R.I. Gen. Laws § 6-13-19

South Carolina: S.C. Code Ann. § 7-5-170

South Dakota: S.D. Codified Laws § 32-12-17.10; § 32-12-17.13

Texas: Tex. Bus. & Com. Code Ann. 35.48

Texas: Tex. Bus. & Com. Code Ann. 35.58; Elec. Code Ann. § 13.004

Utah: Utah Code Ann. § 31A-21-110

Vermont: 9 Ver. Stat. Ann §§ 2030, 2440

Virginia: Va. Code Ann. § 59.1-443.2

Wisconsin: Wis. Stat. § 36.32

West Virginia: W. Va. Code § 17E-1-11.

C. US federal regulations

1. Regulations imposing obligation to provide security

(a) **COPPA regulations**: 16 CFR. 312.8.

(b) **DHS regulations:** Electronic Signature and Storage of Form I-9, Employment Eligibility Verification, 8 CFR. Part 274a (e), (f), (g), and (h).

(c) **FCC Order re pretexting,** April 2, 2007 – In the Matter of Implementation of the Telecommunications Act of 1996: Telecommunications Carriers' Use of Customer Proprietary Network Information and Other Customer Information IP-Enabled Services, CC Docket No. 96-115, WC Docket No. 04-36, April 2, 2007, Paragraphs 33-36; available at http://hraunfoss.fcc.gov/edocs_public/attachmatch /FCC-07-22A1.pdf.

(d) **FDA regulations:** 21 CFR. Part 11.

(e) **FFIEC guidance:** Authentication in an Internet Banking Environment, October 12, 2005, available at www.ffiec.gov/pdf/authentication_guidance.pdf. See also "Frequently Asked Questions on FFIEC Guidance on Authentication in an Internet Banking Environment," August 8, 2006, p. 5, available at www.ncua.gov/letters/2006/CU/06-CU-13_encl.pdf.

(f) **GLB security regulations**: Interagency Guidelines Establishing Standards for Safeguarding Consumer Information (to implement §§ 501 and 505(b) of the Gramm-Leach-Bliley Act), 12 CFR. Part 30, Appendix B (OCC), 12 CFR. Part 208, Appendix D (Federal Reserve System), 12 CFR. Part 364, Appendix B

(FDIC), 12 CFR. Part 568 (Office of Thrift Supervision), and 16 CFR. Part 314 (FTC).

(g) **GLB security regulations (FTC)**: FTC Safeguards Rule (to implement §§ 501 and 505(b) of the Gramm-Leach-Bliley Act), 16 CFR. Part 314 (FTC).

(h) **HIPAA security regulations**: Final HIPAA Security Regulations, 45 CFR. Part 164, adopted by US Department of Health and Human Services on February 20, 2003.

(i) **IRS regulations**: Rev. Proc. 97-22, 1997-1 C.B. 652, 1997-13 I.R.B. 9, and Rev. Proc. 98-25.

(j) **IRS regulations**: IRS Announcement 98-27, 1998-15 I.R.B. 30, and Tax Regs. 26 CFR. § 1.1441-1(e)(4)(iv).

(k) **OFHEO safety and soundness regulation**, 12 CFR. Part 1720, Appendix C – Policy Guidance; Safety and Soundness Standards for Information, available at www.ofheo.gov/Media/Archive/docs/regs/finalssr.pdf.

(l) **OFHEO record retention regulation**, 12 CFR. Part 1732 (Section 1732.6), available at www.ofheo.gov/media/pdf/RecordRetentionfinalreg102706.pdf.

(m)**SEC regulations**: 17 CFR. 240.17a-4, and 17 CFR. 257.1(e)(3).

(n) **SEC regulations**: 17 CFR. § 248.30   Procedures to safeguard customer records and information; disposal of consumer report information (applies

pdf

to any broker, dealer, and investment company, and every investment adviser registered with the SEC).

2. Data disposal / destruction regulations

(a) **FCRA data disposal rules**: 12 CFR. Parts 334, 364.

(b) **SEC regulations**: 17 CFR. § 248.30. Procedures to safeguard customer records and information; disposal of consumer report information (applies to any broker, dealer, and investment company, and every investment adviser registered with the SEC).

3. Security breach notification regulations

(a) **FCC Order re pretexting**, April 2, 2007 – In the Matter of Implementation of the Telecommunications Act of 1996: Telecommunications Carriers' Use of Customer Proprietary Network Information and Other Customer Information IP-Enabled Services, CC Docket No. 96-115, WC Docket No. 04-36, April 2, 2007, paragraphs 26-32; available at http://hraunfoss.fcc.gov/edocs_public/attachmatch /FCC-07-22A1.pdf.

(b) **GLB security breach notification rule**: Interagency Guidance on Response Programs for Unauthorized Access to Customer Information and Customer Notice, 12 CFR. Part 30 (OCC), 12 CFR. Part 208 (Federal Reserve System), 12 CFR. Part 364 (FDIC), and 12 CFR. Part 568 (Office of Thrift Supervision), available at

www.occ.treas.gov/consumer/Customernoticeguid
ance.pdf.

(c) **IRS regulations**: Rev. Proc. 97-22, 1997-1 C.B.
652, 1997-13 I.R.B. 9, and Rev. Proc. 98-25.

D. US state regulations

1. **Insurance – NAIC model regulations**: National
Association of Insurance Commissioners, Standards
for Safeguarding Consumer Information, Model
Regulation.

2. **Attorneys** – New Jersey Advisory Committee on
Professional Ethics, Opinion 701 (2006) available at
www.judiciary.state.nj.us/notices/ethics/ACPE_Opini
on701_ElectronicStorage_12022005.pdf.

E. US court decisions

1. In Re *TJX Companies Retail Security Breach
Litigation*, 2007 US Dist. Lexis 77236 (D. Mass.
October 12, 2007) (rejecting a negligence claim due
to the economic loss doctrine, but allowing a
negligent misrepresentation claim to proceed).

2. *Wolfe v. MBNA America Bank*, 485 F.Supp.2d 874,
882 (W.D. Tenn. 2007).

3. *Lorraine v. Markel*, 2007 US Dist. LEXIS 33020
(D. Md. May 4, 2007).

4. *Guin v. Brazos Higher Education Service*, 2006 US
Dist. LEXIS 4846 (D. Minn. Feb. 7, 2006).

5. *American Express v. Vinhnee*, 336 B.R. 437; 2005 Bankr. LEXIS 2602 (9th Cir. December 16, 2005).

6. *Bell v. Michigan Council 25*, No. 246684, 2005 Mich. App. LEXIS 353 (Mich. App. Feb. 15, 2005) (Unpublished opinion).

7. *Inquiry Regarding the Entry of Verizon-Maine Into The InterLATA Telephone Market Pursuant To Section 271 of Telecommunication Act of 1996*, Docket No. 2000-849, Maine Public Utilities Commission, 2003 Me. PUC LEXIS 181, April 30, 2003; available at www.maine.gov/mpuc/orders/2000/2000-849o.htm.

F. US FTC decisions and consent decrees

1. In the matter of the TJX Companies, Inc. FTC File No. 072-3055 (Agreement containing Consent Order, March 27, 2008), available at www.ftc.gov/os/caselist/0723055.

2. In the matter of Reed Elsevier Inc. and Seisint, Inc. FTC File No. 052-3094 (Agreement containing Consent Order, March 27, 2008), available at www.ftc.gov/os/caselist/0523094.

3. *US v. ValueClick, Inc.* Case No. CV08-01711 MMM (RZx), FTC File Nos. 072-3111 and 072-3158 (Stipulated Final Judgment, C.D. Cal. Mar. 17, 2008), available at www.ftc.gov/os/caselist/0723111.

4. In the matter of Goal Financial LLC (Agreement containing Consent Order, FTC File No. 072 3013, March 4, 2008), available at

www.ftc.gov/os/caselist/0723013 [for alleged failure to provide "reasonable and appropriate security" for consumers' personal information in violation of the FTC's Standards for Safeguarding Customer Information Rule and its Privacy of Customer Financial Information Rule (both of which implement provisions of the Gramm-Leach-Bliley Act)].

5. In the matter of Life is Good, Inc. (Agreement containing Consent Order, FTC File No. 072 3046, January 17, 2008), available at www.ftc.gov/os/caselist/0723046.

6. In the matter of Guidance Software (Agreement containing Consent Order, FTC File No. 062 3057, November 16, 2006), available at www.ftc.gov/opa/2006/11/guidance.htm.

7. In the matter of CardSystems Solutions, Inc. (Agreement containing Consent Order, FTC File No. 052 3148, February 23, 2006), available at www.ftc.gov/opa/2006/02/cardsystems_r.htm

8. *United States v. ChoicePoint, Inc.* (Stipulated Final Judgment, FTC File No. 052 3069, N.D. Ga. Jan. 26, 2006), available at www.ftc.gov/os/caselist/choicepoint/choicepoint.htm.

9. In the matter of DSW Inc. (Agreement containing Consent Order, FTC File No. 052 3096, Dec. 1, 2005), available at www.ftc.gov/opa/2005/12/dsw.htm.

10. In the matter of BJ's Wholesale Club, Inc. (Agreement containing Consent Order, FTC File

No. 042 3160, June 16, 2005), available at www.ftc.gov/opa/2005/06/bjswholesale.htm.

11. In the matter of Sunbelt Lending Services, Inc. (Agreement containing Consent Order, FTC File No. 042 3153, Nov. 16, 2004), available at www.ftc.gov/os/caselist/0423153/04231513.htm.

12. In the matter of Petco Animal Supplies, Inc. (Agreement containing Consent Order, FTC File No. 042 3153, Nov. 7, 2004), available at www.ftc.gov/os/caselist/0323221/0323221.htm.

13. In the matter of MTS, Inc. d/b/a Tower records/Books/Video (Agreement containing Consent Order, FTC File No. 032-3209, Apr. 21, 2004), available at www.ftc.gov/os/caselist/0323209/040421agree0323 209.pdf.

14. In the matter of Guess? Inc. (Agreement containing Consent Order, FTC File No. 022 3260, June 18, 2003), available at www.ftc.gov/os/2003/06/guessagree.htm.

15. *FTC V. Microsoft* (Consent Decree, Aug. 7, 2002), available at www.ftc.gov/os/caselist/0123240/0123240.shtm

16. In the matter of Eli Lilly and Company (Decision and Order, FTC Docket No. C-4047, May 8, 2002), available at www.ftc.gov/os/2002/05/elilillydo.htm.

G. US state Attorneys General consent decrees

1. In the matter of Providence Health System-Oregon (Attorney General of Oregon, Assurance of

Discontinuance), September 26, 2006, available at www.doj.state.or.us/releases/pdf/finfraud_providenc e_avc.pdf.

2. In the matter of Barnes & Noble.com, LLC (Attorney General of New York, Assurance of Discontinuance, Apr. 20, 2004).

3. In the matter of Ziff Davis Media Inc. (Attorneys General of California, New York, and Vermont), Assurance of Discontinuance, Aug. 28, 2002), available at www.oag.state.ny.us/press/2002/aug/aug28a_02_att ach.pdf.

H. Country laws

1. **Argentina:** Act 25,326, Personal Data Protection Act (October 4, 2000), § 9; Security Measures for the Treatment and Maintenance of the Personal Data Contained in Files, Records, Databanks and Databases, either non state Public and Private (November 2006).

2. **Australia:** Privacy Act 1988, Act No. 119 of 1988 as amended taking into account amendments up to Act No. 86 of 2006, Schedule 3, Clause 4.

3. **Belgium:**

   (a) Belgian Law of 8 December 1992 on Privacy Protection in relation to the Processing of Personal Data, as modified by the law of 11 December 1998 Implementing Directive 95/46/EC, and the law of 26 February 2003; available at

www.law.kuleuven.ac.be/icri/publications/499C
onsolidated_Belgian_Privacylaw_v200310.pdf.
See Chapter IV, Article 16 (Confidentiality and
security of processing).

(b) See also, 13 February 2001 – Royal Decree
Implementing the Act of December 8, 1992 on
Privacy Protection in relation to the Processing
of Personal Data.

4. **Canada:** Personal Information Protection and
Electronic Documents Act (2000, c. 5), Schedule 1,
§ 4.7.

5. **Czech Republic:** Consolidated version of the
Personal Data Protection Act, Act 101 of April 4,
2000 on the Protection of Personal Data and on
Amendment to Some Acts; available at
http://ec.europa.eu/justice_home/fsj/privacy/docs/im
plementation/czech_republic_act_101_en.pdf See
Articles 15, 27, 44, and 45.

6. **Cyprus:** Law of 2001, amended 2003; available at
www.dataprotection.gov.cy/dataprotection/dataprote
ction.nsf/697e70c0046f7759c2256e8c004a0a49/f8e
24ef90a27f34fc2256eb4002854e7/$FILE/138(I)-
2001_en.pdf. See Article 10(3).

7. **Denmark:** Act on Processing of Personal Data; Act
No. 429 of 31 May 2000, (unofficial English
translation); available at
www.datatilsynet.dk/english/the-act-on-processing-
of-personal-data. See Title IV, Part 11, Sections 41
and 42 (Security of processing).

8. **EU Data Protection Directive**: European Union
Directive 95/46/EC of February 20, 1995, on the

protection of individuals with regard to the processing of personal data and on the free movement of such data (Data Protection Directive), Article 17, available at http://eur-lex.europa.eu/LexUriServ/LexUriServ.do?uri=CEL EX:31995L0046:EN:HTML.

9. **EU Data Protection Directive:** European Union Directive 2006/24/EC of March 15, 2006, on the retention of data generated or processed in connection with the provision of publicly available electronic communications services or of public communications networks and amending Directive 2002/58/EC, available at http://eurocrim.jura.uni-tuebingen.de/cms/en/doc/745.pdf.

10. **Estonia:** Personal Data Protection Act; Passed 12 February 2003 (RT[1] I 2003, 26, 158), entered into force 1 October 2003; available at www.legaltext.ee/text/en/X70030.htm. See Chapter 3, Sections 18-20 (Personal Data Processing Requirements and Security Measures to Protect Personal Data).

11. **Finland:** The Finnish Personal Data Act (523/1999), given on 22.4.1999; available at www.tietosuoja.fi/uploads/hopxtvf.HTM. See Chapter 7, Sections 32-35 (Data security and storage of personal data).

12. **France:** ACT 78-17 of January 6th, 1978 on Data Processing, Data Files and Individual Liberties; Amended by the Act of 6 August 2004 relating to the protection of individuals with regard to the processing of personal data; available at

www.cnil.fr/fileadmin/documents/uk/78-17VA.pdf
See Articles 34 and 35.

13. **Germany:** Federal Data Protection Act as of 15 November 2006; available at www.bfdi.bund.de/cln_030/nn_535764/EN/DataPro tectionActs/DataProtectionActs_node.html_nnn=t rue. See Section 9 (Technical and organisational measures), Section 9a (Data protection audit), and Annex (to the first sentence of Section 9 of this Act).

14. **Greece:** Law 2472/1997 on the Protection of Individuals with regard to the Processing of Personal Data (as amended by Laws 2819/2000 and 2915/2001); available at www.dpa.gr/Documents/Eng/2472engl_all2.doc. See Article 10 (Confidentiality and security of processing).

15. **Hong Kong:** Personal Data (Privacy) Ordinance, December 1996, Schedule 1, Principle 4.

16. **Hungary:** Act LXIII of 1992 on the Protection of Personal Data and Public Access to Data of Public Interest; available at http://abiweb.obh.hu/dpc/index.php?menu=gyoker/r elevant/national/1992_LXIII. See Article 10 (Data Security).

17. **Ireland:** Data Protection Act of 1988; available at www.irishstatutebook.ie/1988/en/act/pub/0025/inde x.html; Data Protection (Amendment) Act 2003; available at www.irishstatutebook.ie/2003/en/act/pub/0006/inde x.html. Informal consolidation of both Acts

available at
www.dataprotection.ie/viewdoc.asp?DocID=796&ad=1. See Section 2.-(1), Security measures 2C, and First Schedule Article 7 (Data Security).

18. **Italy:** Personal Data Protection Code, Legislative Decree No. 196 of 30 June 2003; available at www.garanteprivacy.it/garante/document?ID=311066. See Chapter II (Minimum Security Measures) at Sections 33 (Minimum Security Measures), Section 34 (Processing by Electronic Means), Section 35 (Processing without Electronic Means), Section 36 (Upgrading), and Annex B (Technical Specifications Concerning Minimum Security Measures).

19. **Japan**: Act on the Protection of Personal Information, Law No.57, 2003, Articles 20, 21, 22, and 43

20. **Latvia:** Personal Data Protection Law, amended by Law of 24 October 2002; available at www.dvi.gov.lv/eng/legislation/pdp. See Section 26.

21. **Lithuania** – Law on Legal Protection of Personal Data, 21 January 2003, No. IX-1296, Official translation, with amendments 13 April 2004; available at www.ada.lt/images/cms/File/pers.data.prot.law.pdf. See Chapter 4, Article 24 (Security of Data).

22. **Luxembourg:** DPL approved on 2 August 2002 and published in Memorial A 91 of 13 August 2002. (English version not available).

23. **Malta:** Data Protection Act of December 14 2001 (Act XXVI of 2001), as amended by Act XXXI of 2002, Full entry into force July 15, 2003, available at http://ec.europa.eu/justice_home/fsj/privacy/docs/implementation/malta_en.pdf. See Articles 26 and 27.

24. **Netherlands:** 25 892 - Rules for the protection of personal data (Personal Data Protection Act) (Unofficial translation); available at www.dutchdpa.nl/downloads_wetten/wbp.pdf. See Articles 13-15.

25. **Poland:**

    (a) Act of August 29, 1997 on the Protection of Personal Data, amended January 1, 2004, March 1, 2004, May 1, 2004; available at http://ec.europa.eu/justice_home/fsj/privacy/docs/implementation/poland_en.pdf. See Articles 7, 31, 36, and 39a.

    (b) Ordinance of the Minister for Internal Affairs and Administration of 29 April 2004; documentation of processing of personal data and technical and organizational requirements which should be fulfilled by equipment and computer systems used for processing personal data (Journal of Laws of 1 May 2004).

26. **Portugal:** Act on the Protection of Personal Data (transposing into the Portuguese legal system Directive 95/46/EC of the European Parliament and of the Council of 24 October 1995 on the protection of individuals with regard to the processing of personal data and on the free movement of such

data); available at
www.cnpd.pt/bin/legis/nacional/lei_6798en.htm.
See Chapter II, Section III (Security and
confidentiality of processing), at Article 14
(Security of processing), Article 15 (Special security
measures), Article 16 (Processing by a processor),
and Article 17 (Professional secrecy).

27. **Slovakia:** Act No 428 of 3 July 2002 on personal
data protection; available at
www.dataprotection.gov.sk/buxus/docs/act_no_428.
pdf. See Chapter Two (Security of personal data),
at Section 15 (Responsibility for personal data
security), Section 16 (The security project), Section
17 (Instruction), Section 18 (Confidentiality
obligation), and Section 19 (Personal data protection
supervision).

28. **Slovenia:** Personal Data Protection Act, available
at
http://ec.europa.eu/justice_home/fsj/privacy/docs/im
plementation/personal_data_protection_act_rs_2004
.pdf. See Chapter 3, Articles 24 (Security of
Personal Data), and Article 25 (Duty to Secure).

29. **South Korea**: The Act on Promotion of Information
and Communications Network Utilization and
Information Protection, Etc. Amended by Act No.
7812, December 30, 2005, Articles 28, 29

30. **Spain:**

(a) Organic Law 15/1999 of 13 December on the
Protection of Personal Data; available at
www.agpd.es/upload/Ley%20Org%E1nica%20

15-99_ingles.pdf. See Article 9 (Data security), Article 10 (Duty of secrecy).

(b) Royal Decree 1720/2007, of 21 December, Which Approves the Regulation Implementing Organic Law 15/1999, of 13 December, on the Protection of Personal Data, unofficial translation available at https://www.agpd.es/portalweb/english_resources/common/reglamentolopd_en.pdf. See Articles 79 - 114 (Regarding security measures in the processing of personal data).

31. **Sweden:**

(a) Personal Data Act (1998:204); issued 29 April 1998; available at www.sweden.gov.se/content/1/c6/01/55/42/b451922d.pdf. See Security in processing at Section 30 (Persons who process personal data), Section 31 (Security measures), and Section 32 (The supervisory authority may decide on security measures).

(b) Personal Data Ordinance (1998:1191); issued 3 September 1998, available at www.sweden.gov.se/content/1/c6/02/56/33/ed5aaf53.pdf.

(c) UN Convention on the Use of Electronic Communications in International Contracts – Article 9, available at www.uncitral.org/uncitral/en/uncitral_texts/electronic_commerce/2005Convention.html.

Appendix

32. **UK:** Data Protection Act 1998; available at
www.hmso.gov.uk/acts/acts1998/19980029.htm.
See Article 7 and the Seventh Principle.

ITG RESOURCES

IT Governance Ltd sources, creates and delivers products and services to meet the real-world, evolving IT governance needs of today's organisations, directors, managers and practitioners. The ITG website (_www.itgovernance.co.uk_) is the international one-stop-shop for corporate and IT governance information, advice, guidance, books, tools, training and consultancy.

www.itgovernanceusa.com/infosec.aspx is the information page from our website for information security and ISO27001 resources.

Other Websites

Books and tools published by IT Governance Publishing (ITGP) are available from all business booksellers and are also immediately available from the following websites:

www.itgovernance.co.uk/catalog/355 provides information and online purchasing facilities for every currently available book published by ITGP.

www.itgovernanceusa.com is a US$-based website that delivers the full range of IT Governance products to North America, and ships from within the continental USA.

www.itgovernanceasia.com provides a selected range of ITGP products specifically for customers in South Asia.

www.27001.com is the IT Governance Ltd website that deals specifically with information security management, and ships from within the continental USA.

Pocket Guides

For full details of the entire range of pocket guides, simply follow the links at *www.itgovernance.co.uk/publishing.aspx*.

Toolkits

ITG's unique range of toolkits includes the IT Governance Framework Toolkit, which contains all the tools and guidance that you will need in order to develop and implement an appropriate IT governance framework for your organisation. Full details can be found at *www.itgovernance.co.uk/products/519*.

For a free paper on how to use the proprietary Calder-Moir IT Governance Framework, and for a free trial version of the toolkit, see
www.itgovernance.co.uk/calder_moir.aspx.

There is also a wide range of toolkits to simplify implementation of management systems, such as an ISO/IEC 27001 ISMS or a BS25999 BCMS, and these can all be viewed and purchased online at: *http://www.itgovernance.co.uk/catalog/1*

Best Practice Reports

ITG's range of Best Practice Reports is now at *www.itgovernance.co.uk/best-practice-reports.aspx*. These offer you essential, pertinent, expertly researched information on an increasing number of key issues including Web 2.0 and Green IT.

Training and Consultancy

IT Governance also offers training and consultancy services across the entire spectrum of disciplines in the information governance arena. Details of training courses can be accessed at *www.itgovernance.co.uk/training.aspx* and descriptions of our consultancy services can be found at *http://www.itgovernance.co.uk/consulting.aspx*.

Why not contact us to see how we could help you and your organisation?

Newsletter

IT governance is one of the hottest topics in business today, not least because it is also the fastest moving, so what better way to keep up than by subscribing to ITG's free monthly newsletter *Sentinel*? It provides monthly updates and resources across the whole spectrum of IT governance subject matter, including risk management, information security, ITIL and IT service management, project governance, compliance and so much more. Subscribe for your free copy at: *www.itgovernance.co.uk/newsletter.aspx*.

Lightning Source UK Ltd.
Milton Keynes UK
05 March 2010

151006UK00001B/7/P